LOST & TRIBES LAST DAYS

WHAT MODERN REVELATION
TELLS US ABOUT
THE OLD TESTAMENT

KENT P. JACKSON

ΛΛ ®

DESERET
BOOK

SALT LAKE CITY, UTAH

Library of Congress Cataloging-in-Publication Data

Jackson, Kent P.
    Lost tribes and last days : what modern revelation tells us about the Old Testament / Kent P. Jackson.
        p. cm.
    Includes bibliographical references and index.
    ISBN 1-59038-480-6 (hardbound : alk. paper)
    1. Bible. O.T.—Criticism, interpretation, etc.   2. Book of Mormon—Relation to the Bible.   I. Title.
    BS1171.3.J33 2005
    289.3'2—dc22   2005008842

Printed in the United States of America   72076
Publishers Printing, Salt Lake City, UT

10   9   8   7   6   5   4   3   2

CONTENTS

PREFACE   vii

INTRODUCTION   1

1. BLESSINGS LOST   4

2. THE LAW OF MOSES AND THE GOSPEL   14

3. IS THE OLD TESTAMENT A TESTAMENT OF
   JESUS CHRIST?   29

4. SCATTERING AND GATHERING   41

5. THE GATHERING OF JOSEPH, THE GENTILES,
   AND THE JEWS   50

6. WHERE ARE THE "LOST TEN TRIBES"?   62

7. WHO WROTE ISAIAH?   72

8. HOW TO READ ISAIAH   78

9. THE ROD AND ROOT OF JESSE   91

v

10. JOSEPH SMITH AND THE LORD'S SERVANT
    IN ISAIAH   96

11. NURSING FATHERS AND NURSING MOTHERS   103

12. THE LATTER-DAY DAVID   107

13. THE STICK OF JOSEPH AND THE STICK OF JUDAH   112

14. APOCALYPTIC REVELATION   121

15. ARMAGEDDON   125

16. GOG AND MAGOG   135

17. A MILLENNIAL TEMPLE IN JERUSALEM   141

18. NEBUCHADNEZZAR'S DREAM   149

19. AT ADAM-ONDI-AHMAN   156

20. DREAMS, VISIONS, BLOOD, FIRE,
    AND PILLARS OF SMOKE   161

21. JESUS, MORONI, AND MALACHI   165

    CONCLUSION   175

    SCRIPTURE INDEX   179

    INDEX   187

PREFACE

Latter-day Saints read the Bible differently from the way others read it. That is because the restored gospel through the Prophet Joseph Smith gives us an abundance of new and unique scriptural evidence that sheds light on the Bible, its history, and its teachings. The Book of Mormon, the Doctrine and Covenants, the Pearl of Great Price, the Joseph Smith Translation of the Bible, and the Prophet's sermons and writings all provide new knowledge and perspectives on what is contained in the scriptures of ancient Israel and the early Christian Church. Because we have those additional sources of revealed truth, we rejoice to use them to understand the Bible better.

Illuminating the Bible through the restored gospel is not to "Christianize" or "Mormonize" the Bible, as some have wrongly claimed. In drawing from modern revelation, we are simply using all the sources available to us—indeed, the very best sources. Choosing to do otherwise is bad scholarship, but even worse, it is to be unfaithful to the Restoration and its blessings. The Lord told Joseph Smith, "This generation shall have my word through you" (D&C 5:10), and this is a doctrinal principle that we must take seriously. President Marion G. Romney, in a First Presidency

message in 1981, expressed the matter as follows: "In each dispensation, from the days of Adam to the days of the Prophet
Joseph Smith, the Lord has revealed anew the principles of the
gospel. So that while the records of past dispensations, insofar as
they are uncorrupted, testify to the truths of the gospel, still each
dispensation has had revealed in its day sufficient truth to guide
the people of the new dispensation, independent of the records of
the past. I do not wish to discredit in any manner the records we
have of the truths revealed by the Lord in past dispensations.
What I now desire is to impress upon our minds that the gospel,
as revealed to the Prophet Joseph Smith, is complete and is the
word direct from heaven to this dispensation. It alone is sufficient
to teach us the principles of eternal life."[1]

In using modern revelation to understand ancient scripture,
it is important that we go where the evidence takes us and not
merely impose our own culture and experience on the Bible. For
example, the fact that we meet on Sundays in a three-hour meeting block does not mean that people in the Bible had a similar
schedule of worship. Nor does the fact that we sing European
Protestant-style hymns in four-part harmony mean that our
ancient brothers and sisters did the same. But in the things that
matter most, including history and doctrine, modern revelation
shines a very bright light, and in that light we learn many important things that we could never learn from the Bible alone. Above
all, to use the words of King Benjamin in the Book of Mormon,
we learn that "there shall be no other name given nor any other
way nor means whereby salvation can come unto the children of
men, only in and through the name of Christ, the Lord
Omnipotent" (Mosiah 3:17). Those words were spoken over a
century before the birth of Jesus. Modern revelation teaches us
that Christ was the only means of salvation from the earliest days
of human history. Even before his earthly coming, he was the
focus of the worship of faithful Saints, just as he is today. The

greatest message of the scriptures is that salvation and happiness—both earthly and eternal—are in him. That message is found in all of our standard works, including the Bible, but it is taught with special power and clarity in the light of the restored gospel.

NOTE

1. Marion G. Romney, "A Glorious Promise," *Ensign*, January 1981, 2.

INTRODUCTION

This book is a collection of essays on topics in which the restored gospel sheds significant light on the Old Testament. Not included is Genesis, the part of the Bible most significantly affected by modern revelation. My earlier volume, *The Restored Gospel and the Book of Genesis* (Deseret Book, 2001), deals with that book. In the present volume, I discuss several Old Testament topics that I have thought about for years, some of which have been the subject of many conversations with both students and colleagues at Brigham Young University. Several of the chapters originated from articles or parts of articles that I published elsewhere in the 1980s and 1990s, and I revisit them now with the benefit of additional study and reflection. I am not embarrassed to point out that my mind has changed on some topics. In some cases, I am now more certain of opinions I developed years ago, but in other cases, I am not as sure of things as I once was.

Readers will notice that most of the chapters ask questions, even those that do not have a question mark in the title. In some cases, I am still asking the questions, and my goal has been not to provide answers but to present the questions and all the evidence I know of to answer them. Five of the chapters come from two long articles on difficult topics that I wrote twenty years ago but did not feel at the time that I knew enough about to put into print. Readers will notice the frequent use of such words as *perhaps, maybe,* and *it appears that.* Hopefully, the material in this book will be seen as explorations, not as announcements. Yet even with the uncertainties that come from our limitations in knowledge and understanding, it is important that we know that the Restoration *does* provide clear and unambiguous answers on many topics. Some of the more exotic things that some Latter-day Saints believe, particularly on topics relating to the last days, disagree noticeably with what is in the standard works. This is because those beliefs are based not on scripture but on traditions passed around the Church, in some cases over several generations. A few of those beliefs even have their source in the teachings of other denominations. My goal in this book is to present what the scriptures of modern revelation teach about some Old Testament topics, amplified wherever possible by insights from the magnificent sermons and writings of the Prophet Joseph Smith.

Chapters 1–3 deal with the question of whether the ancient Israelites had the Church of Jesus Christ among them in the same way that we do. Joseph Smith taught that in the days of Moses they had the gospel preached to them. Yet "in his wrath," the Lord soon took the Melchizedek Priesthood out of their midst (D&C 84:25). All the prophets testified of Jesus Christ, because he always was the only means of salvation for all of humankind. But did they do so only with "types and shadows," or did they teach with "plainness," as the Book of Mormon prophets did?

Chapters 4–6 ask questions about the house of Israel, including the scattering and gathering of different branches of the covenant family. What does the restored gospel teach us about who and where the Israelites are today? Where are the "lost ten tribes"? When will they be gathered? Who are the Gentiles?

Chapters 7–11 explore the book of Isaiah and some of its

passages that are particularly illuminated through the Restoration. Does modern revelation have something to say about multiple-author theories of Isaiah? How can we best read Isaiah's writings? What does Isaiah say about the latter days?

The remaining chapters deal with a variety of questions raised in the writings of ancient Israel's prophets. Those questions are on topics that include the identity of the latter-day David, the battles of Armageddon and Gog of Magog, a future meeting at Adam-ondi-Ahman, and a future temple in Jerusalem. Why did Ezekiel prophesy of sticks? What is apocalyptic prophecy, and what does it teach us about the last days? What does the Restoration teach us about Nebuchadnezzar's dream, Joel's prophecies, and Malachi's visions of our own time?

In the explanations presented in these pages, I have attempted to be consistent with the teachings of the scriptures and the prophets. But these chapters are *interpretations*, not the real thing, and I encourage readers to seek answers not here but in the revealed sources themselves. Hopefully this book is sufficiently documented in the standard works that it will serve as an invitation for readers to explore the topics in the scriptures.

I express my thanks to generous Brigham Young University colleagues who read drafts of the chapters in the book and provided important corrections and suggestions. Their insights have been a great blessing to me.

1

BLESSINGS LOST

R eaders of the Bible observe that from the time of Moses to the end of the Old Testament, the Bible depicts a continuous and pervasive apostasy in ancient Israel. Israel's unbelieving spirit that the prophets wrote about during the Mosaic dispensation continued with few interruptions following the rejection of God's higher law at Mt. Sinai.[1]

But the rebellion at Sinai was not the beginning of Israel's wandering from true religion. When the Israelites came out of Egypt, it appears that they already were suffering the effects of hundreds of years of living in a polytheistic environment. The scriptures do not allow us to know with certainty, but it seems that the Israelites already had lost most or all of the religion of their ancestors—Abraham, Isaac, and Jacob. Moses needed to teach it to them from the start. Modern revelation is the key to our understanding of ancient Israel and its religion. Without it, we would not know either what happened in Israel's earliest history or why the events of that period were so important. Joseph Smith taught, "When the Israelites came out of Egypt, they had the gospel preached to them."[2] They also had the Church of Jesus Christ established among them, and, as the Prophet said, "all the ordinances and blessings were in the Church."[3] That would

include the Melchizedek Priesthood[4] and apparently also the ordinances of the temple as we have them today: "For, for this cause I
commanded Moses that he should build a tabernacle, that they
should bear it with them in the wilderness, and to build a house
in the land of promise, that those ordinances might be revealed
which had been hid from before the world was" (D&C 124:38).
During the earlier days of Enoch and Melchizedek, those great
leaders succeeded in establishing Zion among their peoples,
enabling them not only to enjoy the blessings of the fulness of the
gospel but also to be sanctified as individuals and as communities (see Moses 7; JST Gen. 14:25–50). As Joseph Smith taught,
"The building up of Zion is a cause that has interested the people
of God in *every* age. It is a theme upon which prophets, priests,
and kings have dwelt with peculiar delight."[5] Thus when Moses
brought the Israelites out of Egyptian bondage, his desire for them
was no different from that of the earlier prophet-leaders. He
sought to establish Zion among them and to "sanctify" them—to
make them saints in the fullest sense (D&C 84:23). Yet in time
they showed themselves unworthy of the invitation, which
brought dramatic consequences, including a lost opportunity to
establish Zion, a loss of the Melchizedek Priesthood, and a loss of
the fulness of the gospel.

From the Old Testament record, it is difficult to determine the
exact chronology of Israel's apostasy in the days of Moses. Quoting
Paul in Galatians 3:19, Joseph Smith taught, "The law [of Moses,
or the Levitical law] was added because of transgression. What, we
ask, was this law added to, if it was not added to the gospel? It must
be plain that it was added to the gospel, since we learn that they
had the gospel preached to them."[6] It appears, then, that as Moses
delivered the Israelites from Egypt and took them into the wilderness of Sinai, he taught them the gospel and established the Church
of Jesus Christ among them. The Israelites then showed by rebellious actions, some of which are recorded in the books of Exodus

and Numbers, that they were unwilling to live according to the fulness of the gospel.[7] As a consequence, the Melchizedek Priesthood was withdrawn and the law of Moses, administered by the Aaronic Priesthood, was revealed as Israel's system of worship. The resulting religion was centered in Jehovah and taught fundamental principles of his gospel like faith and repentance. Yet it did not teach the fulness of the gospel, nor could it provide the fulness of the gospel's blessings. The accounts in the Bible suggest that these developments happened in a rather short period. But if we had the record of Moses' day in its perfection, perhaps we would see that the processes of teaching the gospel, establishing the Church, and training a people to receive the laws and ordinances of salvation were accomplished only over some time. Similarly, an apostasy with consequences as extreme as those which Israel experienced may have involved more complex circumstances than the acts of rebellion recorded in the Old Testament. If we had a more complete record, perhaps we would see that ancient Israel's experience paralleled that of the early Christian Church some thirteen hundred years later. That Church, from its establishment by Jesus himself, lasted less than seven decades before its apostolic leaders were withdrawn from the earth, along with the priesthood and keys that they held.

The most outspoken critics of the behavior of the Israelites in the centuries after Moses were their own prophets. If we believe their words, we must conclude that as a people the Israelites were unwilling to live up to even fundamental principles of social behavior, let alone the higher challenges of gospel living. The Lord's words in the following passages are typical of the condemnations delivered by the prophets. The Israelites were a "sinful nation, a people laden with iniquity, a seed of evildoers." Their "hands [were] full of blood" (Isa. 1:15), their "lips have spoken lies," "their feet run to evil, and they make haste to shed innocent blood: their thoughts are thoughts of iniquity" (Isa. 59:3, 7). "Ye have all gone astray, every one to his wicked ways" (JST Isa. 2:5). When the Lord "looked down from heaven upon the children of men" and saw those who claimed to worship him, "the Lord answered and said, They are all gone aside, they are together become filthy, thou canst behold none of them that are doing good, no, not one" (JST Ps. 14:2–3). The prophets compared the Israelites with the people of Sodom and with the Canaanite nations that preceded the tribes of Israel in Palestine (see Isa. 1:10; 2 Kgs. 21:9). The Old Testament tells us that Israel eventually received the same fate as Sodom and the Canaanites, and it was for the same reasons (see 2 Kgs. 17:7–23).

Through Ezekiel, the Lord revealed that Israel's apostasy began before Moses and continued after him. While the Israelites were yet in Egypt, God commanded them to put away their false religion, but they refused (see Ezek. 20:5–8). So he took them into the wilderness of Sinai and gave them laws and ordinances that would lead them to life and sanctification (see Ezek. 20:10–12). They rebelled again, so he decreed that they would not enter into the promised land. When he pleaded with the next generation not to follow the example of their parents, "the children rebelled against me: they walked not in my statutes, neither kept my judgments to do them, which if a man do, he shall even live in them" (Ezek. 20:21; see vv. 13–20). Because that generation of Israelites, like their parents, despised God's laws, he finally withdrew from them his offered blessings and gave them instead "statutes that were *not* good, and judgments whereby they should *not* live" (Ezek. 20:25; emphasis added). This remarkable passage, corroborated in modern revelation, tells of the withdrawal of the greater blessings and their replacement with the lesser laws, priesthood, and ordinances of the law of Moses. Jacob in the Book of Mormon added that they were "a stiffnecked people; and they despised the words of plainness, and killed the prophets, and sought for things that they could not understand." Therefore, "God hath taken away his plainness from them, and delivered unto them many things which they cannot understand, because they desired it" (Jacob 4:14).

A LOSS OF PRIESTHOOD BLESSINGS

When an individual or a nation comes out in rebellion against God through disobedience and sin, privileges and blessings are withdrawn. So it was with the Israelites. They were given the burdens of the law of Moses, and the Melchizedek Priesthood and its blessings were taken from them. "Now this Moses plainly taught to the children of Israel in the wilderness, and sought diligently to sanctify his people that they might behold the face of God; but they hardened their hearts and could not endure his presence; therefore, the Lord in his wrath, for his anger was kindled against them, swore that they should not enter into his rest while in the wilderness, which rest is the fulness of his glory. Therefore, he took Moses out of their midst, and the Holy Priesthood also" (D&C 84:23–25).

We should consider carefully what it means to have the Melchizedek Priesthood withdrawn. With the forfeiture of the priesthood came also the loss of its ordinances, as well as the law that Israel would have received: "I will take away the priesthood out of their midst; therefore my holy order, and the ordinances thereof, shall not go before them" (JST Ex. 34:1). The new law, unlike the gospel law, would not contain "the words of the everlasting covenant of the holy priesthood" (JST Deut. 10:2). But "when [Moses] was taken," taught President John Taylor, "the keys went with him; that the Aaronic Priesthood ruled until Christ."[8] Without the higher priesthood, Israel's governing priesthood was that of Aaron, which is a lesser priesthood leading to lesser blessings and fewer opportunities. Israel's temples—first the tabernacle in the wilderness and then the Jerusalem temples built by Solomon, Zerubbabel, and Herod—were of the Aaronic order, and thus "the power of godliness" was absent from their ordinances (D&C 84:21). Without the higher priesthood, those ordinances could not seal in heaven what was done on earth but could only teach, symbolize, and anticipate. Under that system, authority rested with the high priest—the president of the Aaronic Priesthood—who presided over the temple. His keys presided over "the preparatory gospel," including repentance and baptism, and "the law of carnal commandments"—the rules and ordinances that we call the law of Moses. The Lord gave that system of worship to Israel "in his wrath" (JST Ex. 34:1–2; D&C 84:26–27). Without the Melchizedek Priesthood, no one can receive the endowment, no one can be married for eternity, and no one can obtain the gift of the Holy Ghost. Faithful elders and sisters in the Church today enjoy far greater gospel blessings than were generally available among ancient Israelites.

But what of baptism, which is an ordinance of the Aaronic Priesthood? After Moses was taken from Israel, was baptism no longer part of Israel's system of worship? Since baptism was revealed in the first generation of history (see Moses 6:64–66) and was part of the "preparatory gospel" of the Aaronic Priesthood (D&C 84:26–27), it probably was intended to play an important role under the law of Moses, as it did among faithful Christian Saints in the Book of Mormon. But baptism is never mentioned in the Old Testament at all, either in the laws that God revealed to Moses or in the record of Israel's history.[9] It seems likely that at some point in history, baptism became lost, or seriously transformed, because of general apostasy among the Israelites. In Jesus' day, more than a thousand years after Moses, Jews performed the *mikveh,* a ritual washing that may or may not have had its origin in a true ordinance. But this ritual's similarity to baptism is only superficial. Baptism is an ordinance of the atonement of Jesus Christ that symbolizes the Savior's death, burial, and resurrection as well as our own process of spiritual rebirth (see Rom. 6:3–11). The ritual bath of the Jews had another meaning, not centered in Christ. Sometime between the time of Moses and the time of Jesus, true baptism was lost to the Israelites in general, and it probably happened very early. But John taught and performed real baptisms, and he did so by the authority of the keys of the Aaronic Priesthood that he held. As the forerunner of Jesus, John's baptism was not only that of "repentance for the remission of sins" (Luke 3:3), but it was also in anticipation of the laying on of hands for the gift of the Holy Ghost. "I indeed baptize you with water upon your repentance," he said (JST Matt. 3:11), but "one mightier than I cometh, . . . [and] he shall baptize you with the Holy Ghost and with fire" (Luke 3:16).

Although the Melchizedek Priesthood was withdrawn from Israel, there were exceptions. Joseph Smith taught that "all the prophets had the Melchizedek Priesthood and were ordained by God himself."[10] We will look at that topic in chapter 2.

A LOSS OF LIGHT AND KNOWLEDGE

The loss of priesthood blessings was not the only consequence of Israel's rebellion, for the scriptures suggest that significant gospel knowledge was forfeited as well. This was to be expected, because there is a significant link between the priesthood and knowledge of the truth. Indeed, the Melchizedek Priesthood holds "the key of the knowledge of God" (D&C 84:19).[11] Alma taught the important principle that knowledge is withheld or withdrawn from those who do not believe: "He that will harden his heart, the same receiveth the lesser portion of the word. . . . And they that will harden their hearts, to them is given the lesser portion of the word until they know nothing concerning his mysteries" (Alma 12:10–11; see also 3 Ne. 26:9–11). "It is given unto many to know the mysteries of God," Alma taught, "nevertheless they are laid under a strict command that they shall not impart only according to the portion of his word which he doth grant unto the children of men, according to the heed and diligence which they give unto him" (Alma 12:9). Jesus explained this same principle to his disciples when he told them what to teach: "The mysteries of the kingdom ye shall keep within yourselves; for it is not meet to give that which is holy unto the dogs; neither cast ye your pearls unto swine, lest they trample them under their feet" (JST Matt. 7:10). As the prophets of ancient Israel held the higher priesthood while their countrymen were collectively not ready for it, so also it appears that the prophets knew and understood the gospel of their Redeemer while their society remained in relative ignorance. For Israel in general, the doctrinal horizon was the law of Moses, a mere "shadow" of the real thing (Col. 2:17; Heb. 10:1). The scriptures suggest that because they continued in rebellion through most of their history, the light and knowledge concerning Christ that their Book of Mormon contemporaries had and that we have received through revelation in our day was withheld from them. Joseph Smith taught, "When God offers a blessing or knowledge to a man and he refuses to receive it, he will be damned. [Such is] the case of the Israelites . . . , in consequence of which he cursed them with a carnal law."[12] Also, "God cursed the children of Israel because they would not receive the last law from Moses."[13]

The result is quickly apparent. From the time that the law of Moses was revealed until the coming of Jesus in the flesh, there are no explicit references to Jesus and his gospel in the Old Testament, though some passages teach of his work through what the Book of Mormon calls "types" and "shadows" (Mosiah 3:15). Contrast this with the direct and explicit teachings concerning Christ that are found everywhere in modern revelation. The greatest of all the Messianic prophecies in the Old Testament, Isaiah's "Suffering Servant" prophecy in Isaiah 53, does not contribute doctrinally as much as some of the simplest pronouncements concerning Jesus in the words of Nephi, Jacob, Benjamin, Alma, Amulek, or Mormon. Perhaps this can be explained, in part, by the removal of precious truths from the scriptural record. But there is more to it than that. The Joseph Smith Translation was revealed to restore the scriptures "even as they are in [God's] own bosom" (D&C 35:20). It is through the JST that we learn of the Christianity of Adam, Enoch, and Noah. Yet in contrast to the dispensations of the Patriarchs, the JST does not depict a Christian setting for the Mosaic dispensation. To the contrary, in the hundreds of changes that the Prophet made in his inspired revision of the Bible from Exodus to Malachi, none restore to it any direct and open teaching of the gospel of Christ. It is difficult to imagine that gospel truths would not have been restored had they once existed in that section of the Old Testament.

The Book of Mormon provides additional evidence for gospel light being withheld from Israel. About one-third of the book of Isaiah from the plates of brass is found in the Book of Mormon, and it exhibits only slight differences from modern texts. Just as in the Old Testament, in that material the ministry of Jesus is not discussed except in veiled, symbolic images.

We cannot discount the Old Testament's condemnations of Israel by attributing them to rhetorical overkill on the part of the prophets. Israel's apostasy is the consistent and repeated message of the Lord's servants in the Old Testament.[14] As President Gordon B. Hinckley stated, "The burden of their message was a denunciation of wickedness."[15] In contrast, Peter taught the Saints in his day how they "might be partakers of the divine nature" (2 Pet. 1:4), and Joseph Smith urged us, "Go forward, go forward and make your calling and your election sure."[16] Yet the Israelite prophets were compelled to deal almost exclusively with such remedials as 'Stop murdering people,' 'Stop praying to stones and sticks,' and 'Stop oppressing widows and orphans.' If they killed the prophets, who were sent to remind them of the minimal moral requirements of the law of Moses, then obviously they did not follow them to build Zion, to learn the doctrines of the kingdom, or to receive from them the saving and sealing ordinances.

NOTES

1. One objective of the present volume is to explore the meaning of that apostasy and to understand its consequences for ancient Israel. Chapters 1–3 are a single study and should be read together. Issues alluded to in one chapter are discussed more fully in another. Hopefully, these chapters will show what the evidence is in the scriptures and in the teachings of Joseph Smith. Still, many questions will remain.

2. *The Evening and the Morning Star* 2, no. 18 (March 1834): 143. For this article, see Elder B. H. Roberts's comments in Joseph Smith, *History of The Church of Jesus Christ of Latter-day Saints*, ed. B. H. Roberts, 2d ed. rev., 7 vols. (Salt Lake City: The Church of Jesus Christ of Latter-day Saints, 1932–51), 2:4, note. In some of the nineteenth-century sources quoted, grammar and punctuation have been standardized where necessary for readability.

3. Andrew F. Ehat and Lyndon W. Cook, eds., *The Words of Joseph Smith: The Contemporary Accounts of the Nauvoo Discourses of the Prophet Joseph* (Provo, Utah: Religious Studies Center, Brigham Young University, 1980), 10.

4. See John Taylor, *Items on Priesthood* (Salt Lake City: George Q. Cannon and Sons, 1899), 4–5.

5. *Times and Seasons* 3, no. 13 (2 May 1842): 776; emphasis added.

6. *Evening and Morning Star* 2, no. 18 (March 1834): 143; brackets and bracketed text in original.

7. For example, Exodus 32:1–35; Numbers 11:1–34; 14:1–45; 16:1–50.

8. Taylor, *Items on Priesthood*, 14.

9. The Joseph Smith Translation shows no evidence for baptism after the days of Moses, although it shows much evidence for it before.

10. Ehat and Cook, eds., *Words of Joseph Smith*, 59.

11. See also Ehat and Cook, eds., *Words of Joseph Smith*, 38–39.

12. Ehat and Cook, eds., *Words of Joseph Smith*, 247.

13. Ehat and Cook, eds., *Words of Joseph Smith*, 244.

14. Some examples are Jeremiah 6:6–7; Ezekiel 22:2–4, 8–13; Hosea 4:1–2, 11–18; Amos 2:4, 6–8; Micah 6:10–13, 16; Habakkuk 1:2–4; Zephaniah 1:4–6; 2:1–4.

15. Gordon B. Hinckley, "The Dawning of a Brighter Day," *Ensign*, May 2004, 82.

16. Ehat and Cook, eds., *Words of Joseph Smith*, 368.

2

THE LAW OF MOSES
AND THE GOSPEL

It is only with a knowledge of the Atonement that we can understand the law of Moses. In the Bible, we are indebted to the apostle Paul for explaining the Mosaic law in the context of gospel truth, a context that was lost from the Israelites in general long before Paul's time. But it is to modern revelation that we turn to gain the fullest understanding. Better than any other book, the Book of Mormon teaches of the law of Moses, of its origin, its purpose, and its meaning. Without it, no one can really comprehend the religion of ancient Israel.[1]

Alma said, "For behold, the Lord doth grant unto all nations, of their own nation and tongue, to teach his word, yea, in wisdom, all that he seeth fit that they should have" (Alma 29:8). For more than twelve hundred years—from Israel's rebellion at Sinai to Jesus' humble submission at Golgotha—God's covenant people lived under the heaven-given system of worship and government that we call the law of Moses. That law, revealed by a prophet and administered by priesthood authority, served Israel well—not only during periods of faith and enlightenment but also during times of darkness and disbelief. Though a lesser law than that to which it pointed, still it fulfilled well its role to preserve and teach Israel "until Christ" (JST Gal. 3:24). Paul called it a *paidagōgos,* translated "schoolmaster" in the King James Version but actually meaning "attendant" or "custodian." The greater law, the gospel of Jesus Christ, consisted of "a more excellent ministry" and "a better covenant" and "was established upon better promises" (Heb. 8:6). Yet the law by which Israel was governed from the time of Moses to the time of Jesus was still a law of God, established by him in his wisdom for the well-being of his children until the day they could accept the gospel in its fulness.

PRIESTHOOD IN ANCIENT ISRAEL

Modern revelation tells us that Moses taught the Israelites in order to prepare them for the spiritual blessings that come from the fulness of the gospel and the ordinances of the Melchizedek Priesthood. But they rebelled and ultimately lost their opportunities (see chapter 1 in this volume). "Therefore, [God] took Moses out of their midst, and the Holy Priesthood also; and the lesser priesthood continued, which priesthood holdeth the key of the ministering of angels and the preparatory gospel; which gospel is the gospel of repentance and of baptism, and the remission of sins, and the law of carnal commandments, which the Lord in his wrath caused to continue with the house of Aaron among the children of Israel until John" (D&C 84:25–27). The priesthood of ancient Israel is called *Aaronic* after Aaron, its first high priest. It is sometimes called *Levitical* because it was held exclusively by the tribe of Levi. All men of that tribe were entitled to some priesthood authority by lineage, but Israelite families in general had no priesthood at all. Under the Aaronic system, the priesthood passed from father to son as an automatic birthright based solely on inheritance. While an inheritance-based priesthood is foreign to our own experience in the Church today, the logic of it was that it allowed the priesthood and its ordinances to continue even in times of collective unworthiness. Thus the lines of authority and the legitimacy of the Aaronic temple ordinances were valid through all of Israel's history, even in times of apostasy and ignorance.

Within Israel's Aaronic Priesthood there were three offices: high priest, priests, and Levites.[2] When the Lord revealed his system for Israel's priesthood government, he commanded the prophet Moses to set apart his brother, Aaron, as high priest. The high priest presided over the tabernacle (and later the temple), its sacrifices, and the other functions of the priesthood. He was the presiding authority in the Aaronic Priesthood and held its keys. The high priest's position was to pass from father to firstborn son throughout all the generations of Aaron's descendants. It was "forever hereditary, fixed on the head of Aaron down to Zachariah, the father of John."[3] Thus, under normal circumstances, there was to be only one at a time holding the office. The position of high priest of the Aaronic Priesthood should not be confused with that of high priest in the Church today, a Melchizedek Priesthood office that is not the same as the position of high priest in Israel's Aaronic order. At the next level were the priests, the rest of Aaron's male descendants. They performed the sacrifices and fulfilled other priesthood functions under the direction of the high priest. The Levites included all the rest of the men of the tribe of Levi. They were chosen to assist the priests in their duties. Just as with the other two Aaronic Priesthood offices, this was a hereditary position, passed on from father to sons.

The Aaronic Priesthood in the Church today is the same priesthood as that of Old Testament times, because it was restored to Joseph Smith by John the Baptist, the last holder of the keys of that priesthood under the Mosaic dispensation.[4] Yet it functions under an entirely different system today and fills a different purpose. The ancient Aaronic Priesthood system was the hereditary priesthood of Israel under the law of Moses. Our Church today, in contrast, is presided over by the Melchizedek Priesthood and enjoys the fulness of priesthood authority and blessings, with a full understanding of the principles of the gospel. We enjoy today what righteous Saints prior to Moses also had and what the Israelites in the Mosaic dispensation could have possessed if they had remained worthy.

Joseph Smith said, "All the prophets had the Melchizedek Priesthood and were ordained by God himself."[5] John Taylor asked how this could be true, because the revelations (D&C 84:25; JST Ex. 34:1) state that (in Elder Taylor's words) "the Lord took it away with Moses." The conclusion that he suggested makes good sense: "Perhaps the Lord conferred it himself upon some at times whom he had considered worthy, but not with permission for them to continue it down upon others."[6] Years later, President Taylor wrote about "the exception of some prominent prophets who held the Melchizedek Priesthood, as the direct gift of God, without, it would seem, the power to confer it upon others."[7] Stated succinctly, "When [Moses] was taken, the keys went with him."[8] Joseph Smith's phrase "ordained by God himself" seems, as President Taylor suggested, to imply something other than the normal succession of conferring priesthood that we witness in the Church today. If the keys of the Melchizedek Priesthood were taken with Moses, then perhaps later prophets received priesthood, and sometimes even keys, in the same manner that Joseph Smith did—by special dispensation from heavenly messengers. The Prophet taught that Elijah, who lived in the ninth century before Christ, was the last to hold the keys of the priesthood, without which the ordinances cannot "be attended to in righteousness."[9] If the keys had been withdrawn previously with Moses, then Elijah or a recent predecessor may have received authority not by succession but by some kind of direct divine commission. Elder Joseph Fielding Smith added an important historical insight: "We may presume, with good reason, that never was there a time when there was not at least one man in Israel who held this higher priesthood (receiving it by special dispensation) and who was authorized to officiate in the ordinances."[10] If the keys were not taken with Moses, then there must have been a narrow chain of Melchizedek Priesthood holders through the centuries concerning which the scriptures provide no record.[11]

As for the role of the prophets in relation to the Aaronic Priesthood, we should not look at the Church today as the model, with the prophet presiding over the structure of the Church and conducting its business. That is not what we see recorded in the Bible. Prophets in the Old Testament seem to stand outside the hierarchy of the Aaronic system, serving as spiritual and social critics to motivate people inside the system, and in society in general, to stay true to the spirit of the Mosaic law. Perhaps we can look at John the Baptist as a model, at least in his prophetic role. John operated outside the recognized system of Judah's religion. He was not accepted by "the chief priests and the elders of the people" (Matt. 21:23; see vv. 24–27),[12] by the Pharisees and Sadducees (see Matt. 3:7–10 and JST additions), nor by the secular ruler (see Matt. 14:3–10). Though he had a following among common people (see Matt. 14:5), his only relationship to Judah's official religion was to point out its sins and challenge its practitioners to repent (see Matt. 3:7–10). Prophets in the Old Testament, as far as we can determine from their own writings, served in the same way. Jeremiah listed the priests as among the major sources of Israel's apostasy, along with wicked rulers and false prophets (see Jer. 2:8; 5:31; see also JST Ps. 14:4). The prophets Micah (see Micah 3:11) and Zephaniah (see Zeph. 3:3–4) did the same. When Lehi attempted to call Jerusalem to repentance, he had to flee for his life with his family (see 1 Ne. 1–2). Judging from Jesus' words in the New Testament, such persecution, often including murder, seems to have been the all-too-frequent fate of the prophets (see Matt. 23:30–35; Luke 11:47–51; see also Jacob 4:14).[13]

THE LAW OF MOSES

The Nephite prophet Abinadi taught: "And now I say unto you that it was expedient that there should be a law given to the children of Israel, yea, even a very strict law; for they were a stiffnecked people, quick to do iniquity, and slow to remember the Lord their God; therefore there was a law given them, yea, a law of performances and of ordinances, a law which they were to observe strictly from day to day, to keep them in remembrance of God and their duty towards him. But behold, I say unto you, that all these things were types of things to come. And now, did they understand the law? I say unto you, Nay, they did not all understand the law; and this because of the hardness of their hearts; for they understood not that there could not any man be saved except it were through the redemption of God" (Mosiah 13:29–32). For convenience, the law of Moses can be divided into three categories: the Ten Commandments, civil and religious laws, and sacrificial ordinances.

The Ten Commandments are fundamental rules for any community. One modern scholar has called them "a list of things necessary to preserve the tranquil continuation of society."[14] Their principles are eternal and thus predate ancient Israel, yet they are still in force today as part of the higher law of the gospel. They have been repeated (at least in part) in the New Testament (see Matt. 5:21, 27; 15:4),[15] the Book of Mormon (see Mosiah 12:32–36; 13:11–24), and the Doctrine and Covenants (see D&C 42:18–25). In ancient Israel—a theocracy—civil and religious laws were under the same authority.[16] The laws of the Old Testament deal with a wide variety of matters: family affairs, food, property, sanitation, inheritance, crime, social and religious obligations, and so forth. The laws dealing with civil matters were temporary and are not in force in the Church today, but the general principles upon which Israel's religious laws are based form the foundation of God's laws in all generations.

To the Israelites the Lord said: "Ye shall therefore sanctify yourselves, and ye shall be holy; for I am holy" (Lev. 11:44). Holiness, the state of being set apart by righteousness, is a central theme of the Mosaic code, and all of its laws were established to achieve it. Through his system of laws, God set down rules that taught principles of cleanliness, virtue, justice, mercy, diligence, material well-being, and obedience. The aim of many of the laws was to achieve and maintain ceremonial purity, so the worshipers might be set apart (both literally and figuratively) from the world and found clean to enter the sanctuary, which represented the presence of God. Many aspects of laws regarding behavioral and dietary purity were symbolic of greater things and could be understood in a more sublime way by those who could see with faith: as ceremonial purity enabled one to approach with confidence God's earthly symbols, purity of heart enables us to enter the presence of God. The laws taught that no unclean thing could come into the presence of the Lord. No one who was ritually unclean could participate in the tabernacle or temple worship until he or she had undergone the requirements of ritual purification. Even something as mundane as eating provided a valuable teaching tool. Each time one ate there was a strong reminder that one was under covenant with the Lord to observe certain rules that set one apart from others. By faithfully abstaining from certain foods and by eating in a carefully prescribed way, the Israelites had a chance to renew daily their personal commitments to their faith and the principle of holiness that it taught. In all aspects of life, observance of the law kept Israel "in remembrance of God and their duty towards him" (Mosiah 13:30).

SACRIFICES POINTING TO CHRIST

The sacrifices of the law of Moses were the principal temple ordinances of ancient Israel, performed under strict conditions spelled out in the books of Exodus and Leviticus. According to the law of Moses, except in rare instances the sacrifices could be administered only by the priests and only at the appointed location (at the tabernacle, and then at the temple in Jerusalem following its construction). Although there were several kinds of sacrifices, there was one central focus, as was revealed in the days of Adam: "This thing is a similitude of the sacrifice of the Only Begotten of the Father, which is full of grace and truth" (Moses 5:7). The atoning sacrifice of the Lord Jesus Christ was the theme which undergirded the entire idea of sacrifice in the Old Testament, including the sacrifices of the law of Moses. Sacrifice as a function of worship was symbolic of the Atonement, and the sacrifices were meant to teach the principles upon which the Atonement was based. Sadly, after Moses' time apostasy removed that understanding from the worship of Israel, and thereafter the Old Testament is silent regarding the sacrifices' true meaning. It is likely that from the days of Moses until the coming of Jesus, at best only a minority of Israelites were able to see beyond the functions and symbols of the law to the sacred atonement to which they pointed—or had that knowledge revealed to them (see Mosiah 13:32). Yet the Israelites continued the practices, and sacrifice remained in their understanding the means by which holiness was achieved and maintained and sins purged. Fortunately, we have a second witness for Christ that teaches us the meaning of sacrifice and the mission of the Savior; the Book of Mormon provides the fuller perspective.

Under the law of Moses, four categories of animal sacrifice were most important: burnt offerings, well-being (KJV "peace") offerings, sin offerings, and trespass offerings.[17]

Burnt offerings existed centuries prior to Moses. Adam and other righteous Saints down to the time of Moses offered up burnt offerings to commemorate in advance the sacrifice of Christ (see Moses 5:7; Jacob 4:5; also Gen. 8:20; 22:1–18). These were sacrifices of worship that pointed to the Savior. When the law of Moses was revealed, they were retained as part of the law, although we do not know to what extent they differed in function and meaning from the sacrifices of the Patriarchs. Under the Mosaic system, the animal was a male without blemish. The entire animal was burned on the altar to atone for sin in general. Often they were public sacrifices that were performed as part of the regular daily routine of the priests.

Well-being offerings were offerings initiated by worshipers for their own special purposes. Most common among them were thanksgiving offerings (to show special thanks to the Lord; see Lev. 7:12–13, 15; 22:29), vow offerings (to seal a covenant; see Lev. 7:16; 22:18, 21, 23), and free-will offerings (to show willingness to offer freely; see Lev. 7:16; 22:18, 21, 23). These could be males or females from the herd or flock, and only parts of the animal were burned, while the rest was eaten by the worshipers and the priests.

Sin and trespass offerings were for the purpose of achieving reconciliation following violations of the laws of society or of God. When one was guilty of transgressing any of the revealed laws, atonement had to be made by taking the prescribed animal to the priests at the sanctuary. Several different animals were allowable, based on the station and wealth of the offerer. Only parts of the animal were burned; the rest was eaten. Sin and trespass offerings were the same, except that trespass offerings required restitution. The priests offered up the sacrifice in behalf of the worshiper, and through the animal's death, the worshiper was reconciled with the law and thereby became ritually clean.

Not only in the sin and trespass offerings but in all the sacrifices of the law of Moses, we can see a "type"—a pattern of greater things. The offerings of the law had at their foundation the atonement of Jesus Christ, and they pointed toward him the hearts and minds of those who could see with eyes of faith.

JUSTICE AND MERCY IN THE LAW

Amulek taught: "Behold, I say unto you, that I do know that Christ shall come among the children of men, to take upon him the transgressions of his people, and that he shall atone for the sins of the world; for the Lord God hath spoken it. For it is expedient that an atonement should be made; for according to the great plan of the Eternal God there must be an atonement made, or else all mankind must unavoidably perish; yea, all are hardened; yea, all are fallen and are lost, and must perish except it be through the atonement which it is expedient should be made" (Alma 34:8–9). Amulek taught that God "shall not save his people in their sins. . . . he cannot save them in their sins; . . . and he hath said that no unclean thing can inherit the kingdom of heaven; therefore, how can ye be saved, except ye inherit the kingdom of heaven? Therefore, ye cannot be saved in your sins" (Alma 11:36–37). Amulek's repetition emphasizes the point that the violation of commandments makes us unclean and therefore unworthy to return to God. Since only Christ went through life without sin (see Heb. 4:15), no one else—based on his or her own merits—is worthy. That is what Amulek meant when he said that we are all "hardened," "fallen," and "lost" (Alma 34:9). Alma taught: "And thus we see that all mankind were fallen, and they were in the grasp of justice; yea, the justice of God, which consigned them forever to be cut off from his presence" (Alma 42:14). Were we left forever "in the grasp of justice," we would be cut off eternally from the presence of God. But such was not our Father's plan: "And now, the plan of mercy could not be brought about except an atonement should be made; therefore God himself atoneth for the sins of the world, to bring about the plan of mercy, to appease the demands of justice, that God might be a perfect, just God, and a merciful God also" (Alma 42:15).

The word *atonement* can be explained best with the following two definitions: the payment of a penalty or price for wrongdoing, and a reconciliation, that is, the bringing together again of two parties that had been alienated—an "at-one-ment." The atonement of Jesus Christ fits both of these definitions. Because of our sins, we are separated from God and unworthy to enter his presence. Jesus resolved that situation—for those who exercise "faith unto repentance" (Alma 34:16–17)—by taking upon himself the responsibility for our sins and by receiving the consequences that we deserve for them. Through his "infinite and eternal sacrifice" (Alma 34:10), the penalty for sin was paid in full, which made us sinless in the eyes of eternal law and thus worthy—through Jesus Christ—to be reconciled with God and return to his presence. The doctrine of the Atonement is based on two important principles established by God: Justice and Mercy. Justice is the principle that requires an appropriate punishment or penalty for every violation of divine law. Mercy does not entail God simply overlooking or not holding us accountable for our sins, but it provides that the penalty for them can be paid by someone else in our behalf. Under the Father's plan, Mercy is made available by one who is innocent—Jesus Christ—who receives the penalty in place of those who are guilty. Our Heavenly Father has made this plan so his children can repent and change their lives while the standard of Justice is still met. This allows the guilty ones to be made pure, and it satisfies the demands of Justice without having people suffer the eternal consequences themselves—on condition of their faith and repentance. It is the great manifestation of the love of the Father and the Son for us (see John 3:16).

Jesus taught that the law of Moses was fulfilled in him (see Matt. 5:17; 3 Ne. 15:5). To "fulfill" means much more than simply to bring something to an end. The law of Moses was fulfilled in the sense that it was made complete, or filled out. Since the law was something temporary that pointed to a greater reality, its fulfillment could only come when the greater thing to which it pointed came into existence. Thus in important ways, the law of Moses was a great prophecy concerning Jesus and his mission. Nephi taught this principle in the following words: "Behold, my soul delighteth in proving unto my people the truth of the coming of Christ; for, for this end hath the law of Moses been given; and all things which have been given of God from the beginning of the world, unto man, are the typifying of him" (2 Ne. 11:4). Abinadi said that all things pertaining to the law of Moses "were types of things to come" (Mosiah 13:31). Amulek taught: "It is expedient that there should be a great and last sacrifice, and then shall there be, or it is expedient there should be, a stop to the shedding of blood; then shall the law of Moses be fulfilled; yea, it shall be all fulfilled, every jot and tittle, and none shall have passed away. And behold, this is the whole meaning of the law, every whit pointing to that great and last sacrifice; and that great and last sacrifice will be the Son of God, yea, infinite and eternal" (Alma 34:13–14).

All of the law pointed to Christ, as Amulek declared—every "jot," "tittle," and "whit." But that is not to say that for every detail there is a one-to-one correlation between the law and Jesus' mission. Instead, all aspects of the law of Moses taught the fundamental eternal truths upon which the gospel is based: Justice and Mercy. Abinadi characterized the law as being "a very strict law," "a law of performances and of ordinances, a law which they were to observe strictly from day to day, to keep them in remembrance of God and their duty towards him" (Mosiah 13:29–30). Justice requires that for every violation there be an appropriate penalty or punishment. Perhaps no religious system in history has emphasized Justice as strongly as did the law of Moses. The strictness of its demands is shown in the animal sacrifices. Even sins committed unknowingly or accidentally had to be reconciled through animal offerings. There had to be an accounting made for all violations, and punishments were severe.

Alma's words tell of the role of Christ's atonement in applying Mercy to satisfy the demands of Justice: "And now, the plan of mercy could not be brought about except an atonement should be made; therefore God himself atoneth for the sins of the world, to bring about the plan of mercy, to appease the demands of justice" (Alma 42:15). Jesus said, "I, God, have suffered these things for all, that they might not suffer if they would repent; but if they would not repent they must suffer even as I" (D&C 19:16–17). This is the principle of Mercy, which allows one to suffer vicariously the consequences in behalf of another. In the law of Moses, Mercy is taught clearly in the animal sacrifices, which had as their purpose the symbolic removal of sin from individuals and from the community. Under appropriate circumstances for certain violations, vicarious punishment—the sacrifice of animals—was acceptable payment. The innocent animal paid the price in behalf of the guilty person, thus teaching the principle of Christ's atoning Mercy in behalf of others. On the altar of sacrifice, the animal's life was taken, representing the life of the worshiper who had brought the animal to the temple. It received the punishment in place of the worshiper, for "the wages of sin is death" (Rom. 6:23; see also Lev. 17:11). Thus ancient Israelites were symbolically cleansed of their sins, in similitude of the real cleansing from sin that would come through the sacrifice of Jesus Christ.

Paul called the law Israel's "attendant" or "custodian" until Christ (Gal. 3:24), and it was given because Israel would not live the fulness of the gospel (see Gal. 3:19, 24–25). Yet because the Lord loved his people, he gave them a law that would point them toward the gospel, by teaching them the principles upon which the gospel is based: the Justice and Mercy of the Father and the Son. Its purpose was to condition the Israelites to those concepts so they could accept the fulness of the gospel when it was made available to them.

NOTES

1. For the law of Moses in the Book of Mormon, see Kent P. Jackson, "Law of Moses," in *Book of Mormon Reference Companion,* ed. Dennis L. Largey (Salt Lake City: Deseret Book, 2003), 504–6.

2. See Raymond Abba, "Priests and Levites," in *The Interpreter's Dictionary of the Bible,* ed. George A. Buttrick et al. (Nashville: Abingdon, 1962, 1976), 3:876–89.

3. Andrew F. Ehat and Lyndon W. Cook, eds., *The Words of Joseph Smith: The Contemporary Accounts of the Nauvoo Discourses of the Prophet Joseph* (Provo, Utah: Religious Studies Center, Brigham Young University, 1980), 234; spelling, grammar, and capitalization standardized where necessary for readability.

4. See Ehat and Cook, eds., *Words of Joseph Smith,* 65, 156–58, 234–36.

5. Ehat and Cook, eds., *Words of Joseph Smith,* 59. The comparison of the phrase "ordained by God himself" with Doctrine and Covenants 36:2 does not seem to fit in this instance.

6. "Record of the Acts of the Quorum of the Twelve Apostles," 1849 Record Book, 39, Church Archives, The Church of Jesus Christ of Latter-day Saints, Salt Lake City, Utah; cited in Ehat and Cook, eds., *Words of Joseph Smith,* 82–83, n. 3.

7. John Taylor, *Items on Priesthood* (Salt Lake City: George Q. Cannon and Sons, 1899), 9.

8. Taylor, *Items on Priesthood,* 14; see also 8.

9. Ehat and Cook, eds., *Words of Joseph Smith,* 43. The Prophet probably had in mind the keys of the sealing power, not the keys of the Melchizedek Priesthood. But it is not certain from the context.

10. Joseph Fielding Smith, *Doctrines of Salvation,* comp. Bruce R. McConkie, 3 vols. (Salt Lake City: Bookcraft, 1954–56), 3:85.

11. In either case, we know also of David and Solomon, who must have held the Melchizedek Priesthood (see D&C 132:38–39).

12. Ironically, even though he himself was the legitimate holder of the keys of the Aaronic Priesthood and thus had the responsibility to teach and to call Israel to repentance; see Ehat and Cook, eds., *Words of Joseph Smith,* 157, 235, 236.

13. The New Testament provides further examples, of which Jesus himself is the best. Latter-day Saints will recognize that Jesus held higher

priesthood authority than Caiaphas, the high priest at the time of the Savior's ministry. But neither Caiaphas, the priestly families that ruled with him, nor the people in general acknowledged that the priesthood authority of the prophet (Christ) was greater than that of the Aaronic high priest (Caiaphas). The same can be said of Peter and Paul later in the New Testament (see Acts 4:1–21; 22:30–23:10).

14. George E. Mendenhall, personal communication.

15. See also Matthew 19:18–19; Mark 7:10; 10:19; Luke 18:20; Romans 7:7; 13:9; Ephesians 6:2–3; James 2:11.

16. Joseph Smith said regarding civil and ecclesiastical matters, "They were both one; there was no distinction. So it will be when 'the Lord shall be king over the whole earth.'" *Times and Seasons* 3, no. 18 (15 July 1842): 857.

17. The following discussion is based in part on W. S. LaSor, D. A. Hubbard, and F. W. Bush, *Old Testament Survey* (Grand Rapids, Mich.: Eerdmans, 1982), 153–57.

3

IS THE OLD TESTAMENT A TESTAMENT OF JESUS CHRIST?

The Old Testament provides unique opportunities to learn of the Lord and his work, but it also provides unique challenges. The mission and work of Jesus are far less apparent in the Old Testament than in either the New Testament or modern revelation. In contrast, from cover to cover the Book of Mormon is a thoroughly Christian book, openly Christ-centered in every way, and bearing constant testimony to his divinity. But why are Christ and his message not as visible to us in the Old Testament? If he was the God of ancient Israel, as we learn in the Book of Mormon (see 3 Ne. 15:5), why is the Old Testament not a Christian book in the same way that the Book of Mormon is? To attempt to arrive at an answer, we will look at three important issues: the ongoing apostasy of the Israelites and its consequences, the nature and intent of the Old Testament itself, and the removal of parts of the ancient record. We will explore to what extent the Old Testament teaches of Christ and bears testimony to his redeeming mission and to what degree it can be called, like our other scriptures, a "testament of Jesus Christ."

From the outset, it needs to be clear that the question of what ancient people knew of Christ is a historical issue and not a matter of doctrine. It is not a question of whether they needed the gospel or could be saved independently of Jesus. Joseph Smith taught that "all that were ever saved were saved through the power of this great plan of redemption, as much so before the coming of Christ as since. If not, God has had different plans in operation (if we may so express it) to bring men back to dwell with himself. And this we cannot believe."[1] The gospel of Jesus Christ always was the only means of salvation and the only true and living religion on earth. In the times and places where it was available, the ancient Saints enjoyed the blessings of its truths and ordinances.

APOSTASY IN ISRAEL

An important factor that contributes to Christian things not being readily apparent in the Old Testament is the ongoing apostasy of ancient Israel, as observed in chapter 1. Moses established the Church of Jesus Christ among his people and taught them the gospel.[2] Yet the Bible portrays the Israelites as generally rebellious and disobedient from the time of Moses to the time of Jesus (e.g., Acts 7:51–53).[3] As a result, they did not enjoy the blessings that the Lord's Saints have enjoyed in other dispensations. Just as the higher priesthood was withheld from them (see D&C 84:25; JST Ex. 34:1), so also was a knowledge of the gospel as we enjoy it today. That is reflected in the limitation on plain teachings of Christ in the Old Testament.

THE INTENT OF THE OLD TESTAMENT

The nature and function of the Old Testament may provide other reasons why gospel things are not as apparent in it as in our other scriptures. Our Old Testament is the book of the Israelites of the Mosaic dispensation, and thus its content was determined by the limitations of the law of Moses and by Israel's level of faith. Not surprisingly, its focus is on matters pertaining to this earth and not on celestial things. For the most part, the Old Testament's rewards and punishments are material and temporal—good crops, large families, peace, and protection from foreign armies. In the Old Testament, the great climax and culmination of God's work is the Millennium, not the exaltation and eternal life of the Saints. Eternal rewards are rarely mentioned, and even life after death is alluded to only a few times, and not clearly (e.g., Isa. 26:19; Dan. 12:2).

Inasmuch as the prophets held the Melchizedek Priesthood, as Joseph Smith taught,[4] we can suggest that their wives and closest associates similarly enjoyed knowledge and blessings not generally available to others. Thus from time to time—or continuously—there may have been a Church of Jesus Christ among the ancient Israelites, with members who knew and lived his gospel while their countrymen did not. Perhaps they existed in secret, as did Alma's Church in the Book of Mormon (see Mosiah 18; 23–24). But we do not have a written record of Christians in ancient Israel and Judah, and if they existed, it is likely that their record never was contained in the collection we call the Old Testament, nor were the teachings of the prophets to them. Our Old Testament shows every indication of being a book directed to, and recorded for, the Israelite nation in general—not the Saints who may have lived among them. The words of the prophets in the Bible are their public pronouncements to their whole society, not their private teachings to those who had risen above the sins of their generation. That may explain to some degree why the Old Testament is not, and perhaps never was, a Christian book in the same way that the Book of Mormon is.

PLAIN AND PRECIOUS THINGS

We do not possess the history of the Lord's ancient people or the writings of their prophets in their complete and original form. Nephi saw in vision that when the record of the ancient prophets

went forth, it was pure (see 1 Ne. 13:24–25). But "plain and precious parts" were removed from it and from the message that it
contained (see 1 Ne. 13:26–28). Joseph Smith said that he
believed in the Bible "as it ought to be, as it came from the pen of
the original writers."[5] We believe it to be the word of God "as far
as it is translated correctly" (Article of Faith 8), with "translated"
seemingly referring to the entire process of transmission from
original manuscripts to modern-language translations. The Book
of Mormon provides evidence of prophetic teachings not included
in the present biblical canon, because it alludes to, or even quotes
from, ancient Old World prophets whose writings we do not have.
Words attributed to Joseph Smith ascribe changes in the Bible to
three categories of individuals: "ignorant translators," "careless
transcribers," and "designing and corrupt priests."[6] Those who
have struggled to learn a second language or who have made typo-
graphical errors can sympathize with, and overlook, the imperfec-
tions of those who fall into the first two categories (see 3 Ne.
23:7–13). But the third implies a deliberate, calculated effort to
change the revelations of God. Nephi wrote about such efforts,
explaining that "after the book hath gone forth through the hands
of the great and abominable church, that there are many plain and
precious things taken away from the book, which is the book of
the Lamb of God" (1 Ne. 13:28). The Lord warned Moses of the
suppression of parts of scripture, saying that the day would come
when men would "esteem [his] words as naught and take many
of them" from the book which Moses would write (see Moses
1:41). Moses' encounter with the devil, restored in the Joseph
Smith Translation, is a specific example of something deliberately
removed "because of wickedness" (Moses 1:23). It appears from
Nephi's description that "the book of the Lamb of God" (1 Ne.
13:28) refers to both the Old and the New testaments. While the
New Testament likely suffered alterations in the first century after
Christ, changes in the Old Testament probably took place several

hundred years before that. Old Testament manuscripts from the time of Jesus and as much as two centuries earlier are different in only very small ways from the later medieval manuscripts from which modern Bibles, including the King James Version, were translated. This means that any changes made in the Old Testament were made centuries before Christ.

The gospel of Jesus Christ was revealed in the beginning of time, as modern revelation testifies. Those who believe that Joseph Smith was a prophet believe that Adam was a Christian (see Moses 6:51–62), that he was baptized (see Moses 6:64–66), and that he held the holy priesthood (see D&C 107:40–42; Abr. 1:2–3). Animal sacrifice was revealed from the beginning to symbolize the atoning sacrifice of Jesus (see Moses 5:5–8). Adam and Eve taught the gospel of Christ to their children (see Moses 5:9–12). Their descendants, such as Enoch and Noah, believed in Christ, worshiped the Father in his name, and preached faith in his atonement, repentance, baptism in similitude of his death and resurrection, and the laying on of hands for the gift of the Holy Ghost (see Moses 7:10–11; 8:23–24). Abraham was a Christian, he knew the plan of salvation, and, as the Savior himself said, Abraham rejoiced to see the distant coming of Jesus Christ in the flesh (see Abr. 3:22–28; John 8:56; JST Gen. 15:12). Through modern revelation, we also know that Moses knew Christ, that he understood the gospel, and that he knew of Christ's role as Creator and Redeemer (see Moses 1:6, 32–33; 4:1–4; Mosiah 13:33). But none of these realities are in the Bible. We know that they are true because they were revealed to the Prophet Joseph Smith, mostly as part of the Joseph Smith Translation of the Bible, a process of restoring knowledge that was "taken from the Bible or lost before it was compiled."[7] The absence of these truths from the Old Testament makes it less a witness for Christ than it would be had they been preserved in it. But, as the Lord promised Moses concerning the work of Joseph Smith, "I will raise up another like unto thee; and they shall be had again among the children of men—among as many as shall believe" (Moses 1:41).

In the context of these restored truths, an observation is in order. All of these evidences of ancient knowledge of Christ pertain to the time from Adam to Moses. As we have seen, from the time of Moses on, the Old Testament does not present evidence that the ancient Israelites as a whole knew of Christ or had his gospel taught to them in plainness. The Joseph Smith Translation, despite hundreds of changes, does not reveal Christianity in the Mosaic dispensation, and the early chapters of the Book of Mormon suggest that at least by the time of Lehi, Jesus and his gospel were not known among the mainstream of ancient Israelites.[8] The Book of Mormon presents additional evidence, but its meaning is uncertain. Abinadi taught, "Yea, and even all the prophets who have prophesied ever since the world began—have they not spoken more or less concerning these things? Have they not said that God himself should come down among the children of men, and take upon him the form of man, and go forth in mighty power upon the face of the earth? Yea, and have they not said also that he should bring to pass the resurrection of the dead, and that he, himself, should be oppressed and afflicted?" (Mosiah 13:33–35). What Abinadi did not tell us is if those prophets' words were recorded in the Bible and if they taught in "plainness" about Christ or in veiled "types" and "shadows." The example Abinadi gave was Isaiah 53, the great Suffering Servant prophecy. It is the Old Testament's finest prophecy of the earthly ministry of Jesus, yet with its allusions and images it can be understood only by those who know its message from reading the New Testament or the Book of Mormon (see Mosiah 14:1–12). Perhaps this is the kind of testifying of Christ that Abinadi had in mind. In the Book of Mormon we have references to four Old World prophets whose teachings were recorded on the plates of brass and who foretold aspects of the coming of Jesus. Nephi stated that "the God of Abraham, and of Isaac, and the God of Jacob, yieldeth himself . . . to be lifted up, according to the words of Zenock, and to be crucified, according to the words of Neum, and to be buried in a sepulchre, according to the words of Zenos" (1 Ne. 19:10; see also vv. 11–17). Nephi cited Zenos to state that the people of Jerusalem would "crucify the God of Israel" and despise "the Holy One of Israel" (1 Ne. 19:13, 14). Nephi son of Helaman said that Zenos, Zenock, and Ezias spoke of the coming redemption through the Son of God (see Hel. 8:19–20), and Mormon reported that Zenos and Zenock foretold destructions that would accompany Christ's death (see 3 Ne. 10:14–16). Unfortunately, those brief accounts, related in the Book of Mormon in the words of other people, do not allow us to know whether the four prophets' thoughts on the plates of brass were explicit in their teachings or were couched in symbolic language.[9] More explicit references to Christ are found in Alma's sermon about prayer, in which he quoted from Zenos and Zenock. Zenos stated: "And thou didst hear me because of mine afflictions and my sincerity; and it is because of thy Son that thou hast been thus merciful unto me, therefore I will cry unto thee in all mine afflictions, for in thee is my joy; for thou hast turned thy judgments away from me, because of thy Son" (Alma 33:11). And Zenock stated: "Thou art angry, O Lord, with this people, because they will not understand thy mercies which thou hast bestowed upon them because of thy Son" (Alma 33:16). We understand these passages because we know the gospel, but we can only wish that we had more context to know what other things those prophets wrote and how ancient Israelites understood them. Were the people of Israel and Judah even aware of the writings of those prophets? Lehi, a faithful worshiper of Jehovah and a prophet himself, presumably did not have those words until they were acquired from Laban on the plates of brass.

We do not know when the four prophets lived. Nephi son of Helaman reported that Ezias, Zenock, and Zenos were after Abraham (see Hel. 8:19–20), and Mormon wrote that Zenos and

Zenock were ancestors of the Book of Mormon peoples (see 3 Ne. 10:16). Perhaps they lived prior to Moses. Maybe, as Elder Orson Pratt suggested, Ezias was the Esaias in Jethro's line of authority who received the priesthood "under the hand of God" and was blessed by Abraham (see D&C 84:12–13).[10] And yet perhaps they were Israelite or Judahite prophets of later generations. In any case, they knew the mission of Christ and testified of it, whether in "plainness," like the Book of Mormon prophets, or in "types" and "shadows," like Isaiah and other Old Testament prophets.

WERE THE ISRAELITES CHRISTIANS?

The Book of Mormon is the record of a colony of Israelites who left Palestine to escape the evil behavior of their generation and the sad fate that awaited them. The early part of their record shows that Lehi and his family, though honorable people, knew little of Christ before Lehi's prophetic call. Yet in the course of time they were the recipients of revelations that taught them the identity of their Messiah; his name, Jesus Christ; the nature of his redemptive mission; and the purpose and power of his atonement.[11] Jacob reported how his people learned of Jesus: "We also had many revelations, and the spirit of much prophecy; wherefore, we knew of Christ and his kingdom, which should come" (Jacob 1:6). For most of the history of the children of Lehi, there were groups among them who lived in such a manner that their prophets could make known to them the saving work of Jesus Christ. Yet because they were Israelites under the Mosaic dispensation, they were commanded to adhere to the law of Moses until Christ's coming. They did this, however, with the full perspective of the gospel, recognizing that the law was dead to them because they possessed the greater light and knowledge of Christ (see 2 Ne. 25:25–27). With few exceptions, such does not appear to have been the case with their fellow Israelites in Palestine.

It is not clear to what extent the earliest Israelites understood the intent of the law of Moses. When it was first revealed, its connection with Jesus' ministry may have been explicit. But perhaps even then it was veiled in "types" and "shadows" as we see it now. The descriptions of laws and sacrifices in Exodus and Leviticus make no mention of Jesus, nor do they suggest that the sacrifices pointed to a greater sacrifice. Was that always the case? Since the law was revealed by the Lord "in his wrath" because Israel refused to receive greater things (D&C 84:24), were they unworthy even to learn the true meaning of their "performances" and "ordinances" (Mosiah 13:30)? Or did the Lord veil knowledge from their understanding to challenge them to find Christ through the light of faith (see Jacob 4:14)? It appears that at an early date which we cannot determine now, whatever the Israelites had known of Christ became obscured from their view in general, and through most of their history they performed the sacrifices and other observances without an understanding of their true intent. There is no question that by the time of John and Jesus such was the case. But the obscuring of the law probably took place centuries earlier, likely during Israel's first generations. Laman and Lemuel, Jerusalemites of the early sixth century before Christ, justified their rebellion by claiming that their countrymen were "a righteous people; for they kept the statutes and judgments of the Lord, and all his commandments, according to the law of Moses" (1 Ne. 17:22). Ironically, they probably were correct in their assessment that the Jews "kept the statutes and judgments" of the law. The Israelite prophets acknowledged that the people did, but they pointed out that such observance did not constitute righteousness nor love of God. In fact, because of Israel's sins, God condemned their sacrifices, festivals, and other observances (see Isa. 1:10–15; Jer. 6:20; Hosea 8:12–13; Amos 5:21–23). Obviously, despite their adherence to the precepts of the law, the message of Christ was lacking from their worship. "They ignored the heart of the Mosaic law while dressing its bones."[12]

But in spite of all this, the message of Christ was not really absent from the law of Moses, nor from the prophets. The Old Testament teaches primarily by bad examples, but there are also examples of good people doing good things, including Naomi, Hannah, Jonathan, Jesse, Naboth, the handmaid of Naaman's wife, Jehoiada, Baruch, and undoubtedly thousands of others. The limitations on their knowledge and opportunities were not of their own making but the result of the generations in which they lived. With justice, mercy, and forgiveness central to the religion of pious Israelites, faith and repentance were powerful forces that motivated the spiritual lives of many people. In the Old Testament, those principles are embodied in the person and character of Israel's God, Jehovah. Worshipers of Jehovah were worshipers of Jesus Christ, even if they did not know him by that name and in that role. Similarly, many honorable people anticipated a Messiah who would fulfill God's will, even though they did not know fully what he would do and who he would be. Faith in Jehovah was possible for ancient Israelites because Jehovah's power was sufficient to save Israel from every enemy. Repentance was possible because his arms of mercy were ever extended to those who forsook their sins and came unto him. Sincere Israelite worshipers who knew nothing of Jesus Christ understood both faith and repentance and saw them as the foundations of their relationship with a merciful God—even if they did not know the true source of their salvation. By teaching Jehovah's love and mercy and bearing testimony of him, all of the prophets were testifying of Christ, as the Book of Mormon says they did (see Jacob 4:4–5; 7:11). As such, the Old Testament is indeed a testament of Jesus Christ. Perhaps those who could see beyond the symbols with an eye of faith would have seen Jehovah himself as the fulfillment of the law of Moses. Perhaps they would have seen, as did

John the Baptist, that Jesus of Nazareth was God's unblemished offering in their behalf: "Behold the Lamb of God, which taketh away the sin of the world" (John 1:29).

"Wherefore then serveth the law?" "Ordained by angels," it was revealed from the heavens to serve Israel's needs until the generation would come "to whom the promise was made"—the promise of Christ's mortal ministry (Gal. 3:19). The law of Moses and Israel's system of worship, however limited, were blessings intended to sustain Israel until better things could be revealed. A comparison of ancient Israel with the Church established by Jesus and his New Testament apostles may help us understand the Old Testament better. Although apostasy precludes people from enjoying a fulness of gospel knowledge, in both cases a remnant of the fulness remained after the fall of the Church that was sufficient to bless the people with standards of belief and behavior greater than those enjoyed by others of their day. In ancient Israel, the Lord left behind a government (the Aaronic Priesthood), a system of laws (the law of Moses), and prophets to continue to serve the Israelites during their generations of diminished light. In Christianity, the New Testament was the remnant that the Lord left behind to sustain his children until the Restoration, providing them the fundamentals of the gospel and the testimony of Jesus. The law and the prophets were to the Israelites what the Bible was to Christians before 1820, the gift of a loving Heavenly Father to prepare his children for greater revelations to come (see JST Gal. 3:24–25). Some Israelites would be fortunate to live at the time when the promises were fulfilled and would hear and accept the gospel during Jesus' mortal ministry. Many more would need to receive it through the ministry of his servants in the spirit world. Those who in this life lived up to all the knowledge they had will likely welcome and embrace the fulness of the gospel there (see D&C 137:5–9).

NOTES

1. *The Evening and the Morning Star* 2, no. 18 (March 1834): 143. See Joseph Smith, *History of The Church of Jesus Christ of Latter-day Saints,* ed. B. H. Roberts, 2d ed. rev., 7 vols. (Salt Lake City: The Church of Jesus Christ of Latter-day Saints, 1932–51), 2:4, note. In the nineteenth-century sources cited, spelling and punctuation have been standardized where necessary for readability.

2. Ibid.

3. See the references in chapter 1.

4. Andrew F. Ehat and Lyndon W. Cook, eds., *The Words of Joseph Smith: The Contemporary Accounts of the Nauvoo Discourses of the Prophet Joseph* (Provo, Utah: Religious Studies Center, Brigham Young University, 1980), 59.

5. Ehat and Cook, eds., *Words of Joseph Smith,* 256.

6. Smith, *History of the Church,* 6:57. The origin of the words is not known; the original account is in Ehat and Cook, eds., *Words of Joseph Smith,* 256.

7. Dean C. Jessee, ed., *The Papers of Joseph Smith, Vol. 1: Autobiographical and Historical Writings* (Salt Lake City: Deseret Book, 1989), 372.

8. See Kent P. Jackson, "The Beginnings of Christianity in the Book of Mormon," in *The Book of Mormon: The Keystone Scripture,* ed. Paul R. Cheesman (Provo, Utah: Religious Studies Center, Brigham Young University, 1988), 91–99.

9. Zenos's prophecy in Jacob 5 is entirely allegorical.

10. George Reynolds, *A Dictionary of the Book of Mormon, Comprising Its Biographical, Geographical and Other Proper Names* (Salt Lake City: Jos. Hyrum Parry, 1891), 118.

11. See the discussion of this restoration of the gospel to Lehi and his children in Jackson, "The Beginnings of Christianity in the Book of Mormon," 91–99.

12. Richard D. Draper, personal communication.

4

SCATTERING AND GATHERING

As Moses prepared the Israelites to enter into and take possession of the land of Canaan, he announced: "Behold, I set before you this day a blessing and a curse; a blessing, if ye obey the commandments of the Lord your God, which I command you this day: And a curse, if ye will not obey the commandments of the Lord your God, but turn aside out of the way which I command you this day" (Deut. 11:26–28). Among the great blessings that were promised to Israel was the inheritance in a choice land. Canaan was to be the Israelites' homeland under the stipulations of the covenant that God had made with their forefathers (see Gen. 13:14–15, 17; 15:18; 17:8; JST Gen. 14:40). As the Lord told Abraham concerning his descendants, it would be their promised land "which I will give unto thy seed after thee for an everlasting possession, when they hearken to my voice" (Abr. 2:6). As long as they remained faithful to the covenants that they had made with the Lord at Sinai, the land would be theirs. But if they would fall into sin and apostasy, they would be removed from it and scattered among the nations. "When thou shalt beget children, and children's children, and ye shall have remained long in the land, and shall corrupt yourselves, and make a graven image, or the likeness of any thing, and shall do evil in the sight of the

Lord thy God, to provoke him to anger: I call heaven and earth to witness against you this day, that ye shall soon utterly perish from off the land whereunto ye go over Jordan to possess it; ye shall not prolong your days upon it, but shall utterly be destroyed. And the Lord shall scatter you among the nations, and ye shall be left few in number among the heathen, whither the Lord shall lead you" (Deut. 4:25–27). Among Old Testament and Book of Mormon prophets alike, the inheritance in a promised land was one of the major issues of their covenant theology, and thus in a powerful way, the land of inheritance was the token of God's covenant with his people. It is therefore not surprising that God's displeasure with his people in the Old Testament was signified by their expulsion from the land. And in the prophetic future view, return to the covenants would ultimately lead to return to the promised land.

THE SCATTERING

In 922 B.C., the united kingdom of David and Solomon was divided into two nations—Israel in the north, consisting of the northern ten tribes, and Judah in the south, consisting of Judah and Benjamin. Ephraim and Manasseh were probably the most populous tribes in Israel, a nation that is depicted in the Bible as being in virtually uninterrupted apostasy throughout its history. All twenty of the kings of Israel are identified in the Old Testament as wicked. In a series of deportations beginning during the reign of Menahem (745–738 B.C.) and culminating in the destruction of Israel's capital city Samaria in 721 B.C., thousands of largely paganized Israelites were taken from Palestine and relocated in other parts of the Assyrian empire.[1] Our sources of information for those deportations include the biblical accounts (2 Kgs. 15–17), their parallels in the annals of the Assyrian kings,[2] and additional references in the writings of Old Testament and Book of Mormon prophets (e.g., Jer. 32:37; 2 Ne. 10:20–22). The only scriptural reference that we possess concerning the immediate geographical destination of the deportees is found in 2 Kings 17:6, in which we are told that the inhabitants of Samaria were relocated "in Halah and in Habor by the river of Gozan, and in the cities of the Medes." Archaeological evidence—Israelite personal names in Assyrian documents—attests to the assimilation of members of the northern tribes into Mesopotamian society.[3]

Another major Israelite group whose scattering is attested scripturally is the family of Lehi. The Book of Mormon relates the account of God's directing Lehi and his people to the western hemisphere as a branch of Israel with an important destiny. The book attests that they were descendants of Joseph, and Lehi's descent from Manasseh is specified in one passage (Alma 10:3).[4] The fact that the Mulekites and Zoram, the servant of Laban, became one with Lehi's children suggests that the blood of Judah was mixed with that of Joseph in the people of the Book of Mormon. Lehi's descendants, the indigenous peoples of the Americas and the Pacific islands, had some among them who retained their Israelite identity and the knowledge of their origin for a thousand years. Yet they have lost the knowledge of their heritage now, except for those who have found it in the doctrines of The Church of Jesus Christ of Latter-day Saints.

The scattering of the Jews is the best known of all in both sacred and secular history. Beginning perhaps as early as the eighth century before Christ, some Jews began to leave their ancestral land for other locations. The Jewish exile in Babylonia, following the conquest of Judah and destruction of Jerusalem in 587 B.C., is described in the Bible and is well established through extrabiblical sources.[5] By the time of Jesus, probably two-thirds or more of all Jews lived outside Palestine, with Jewish communities scattered throughout the Mediterranean region and the Near East. As a result of the destruction of Jerusalem by the Romans in A.D. 70 and the Second Jewish Revolt in A.D. 132–35, Jews fled or were

deported from Palestine in large numbers. Eventually large popu-
lations grew in scattered locations in Europe and elsewhere. Of
the three major branches of Israel discussed here—the northern
ten tribes, the descendants of Lehi, and the Jews—the Jews alone
have retained a knowledge of their origin and identity. Yet in the
gospel sense, they too are separated from the covenants that God
made with their forefathers, excepting those who have become
members of The Church of Jesus Christ of Latter-day Saints.

THE GATHERING

Because a promised land is one of the blessings of righteousness, the gathering cannot take place without repentance and
conversion. Jesus taught, "And it shall come to pass that the time
cometh, when the fulness of my gospel shall be preached unto
them; and they shall believe in me, that I am Jesus Christ, the Son
of God, and shall pray unto the Father in my name. . . . Then will
the Father gather them together again, and give unto them
Jerusalem for the land of their inheritance" (3 Ne. 20:30–31, 33).

Many of the prophecies of Israel's gathering employ the use of
powerful metaphors—words denoting one object or idea used in
place of another to suggest a likeness between them. In the scriptures, those literary devices are used abundantly to describe the
scattering and gathering of Israel. Thus we read of sheep, sheep-
folds, and shepherds,[6] grape vines, olive trees, and fig trees,[7]
hunters and fishers (see Jer. 16:16–17), sticks (see Ezek.
37:15–24), hearts of stone and flesh,[8] the maimed, the halt, and
the blind (see Luke 14:16–24), nursing fathers and nursing mothers (see Isa. 49:22–23), husbands, wives, harlots, children,[9] dry
bones, highways, ensigns, and promised lands.[10] By the use of
these images, the past, present, and future of Israel are described
in words that are at once both prophetic and poetic.

Throughout history, the Lord has brought his Saints together in order to make all of the gospel blessings available to them. Unquestionably there is strength in numbers—strength in terms of safety, sharing of talents, availability of leadership, and so forth. The greatest blessings available to gathered Saints are those of stakes and especially of temples, in which the sacred covenants once established between God and the ancient Patriarchs are now established between God and his Saints individually. Joseph Smith taught that "the main object" of gathering "the people of God in any age of the world" was to "build unto the Lord an house whereby he could reveal unto his people the ordinances of his house and glories of his kingdom and teach the people the ways of salvation."[11] In the beginning of our own dispensation, the physical gathering was one of the top priorities of the Lord's servants. Now Saints are encouraged to build Zion wherever they are—not because the purposes for gathering are no longer realities but in order to realize those purposes in all parts of the earth among all people. Where faithful Saints are, that is where Zion is. Thus Brazil is Zion, the promised land and gathering place for the Brazilians, Africa is Zion, the promised land and gathering place for the Africans, and so forth throughout the earth. President Spencer W. Kimball taught: "The gathering of Israel consists of joining the true church and their coming to a knowledge of the true God. . . . Any person, therefore, who has accepted the restored gospel, and who now seeks to worship the Lord in his own tongue and with the Saints in the nation where he lives, has complied with the law of the gathering of Israel and is heir to all of the blessings promised the Saints in these last days."[12] The administrations of recent presidents of the Church have been characterized by the establishment of stakes in many countries of the earth, and temples are being built in many locations. It should not surprise us if this work continues at an even faster pace in the coming decades. The Lord's children are being gathered to the covenants of the gospel. They are being gathered to the family of Israel. They are being gathered home to the true faith and the true Church. Though they are not being relocated, they are being gathered nonetheless—in a very real way. The Millennium will be the great day of physical relocation, for the scriptures teach that it will be in that time that Judah and all of Israel will be gathered to promised lands (see D&C 133:25–35; 3 Ne. 20:30–33).

As the scriptures often describe the gathering by using metaphors of sheep returning to their fold, perhaps in some prophecies even the concept of returning to the land is a metaphor to describe the gathering to gospel covenants. In any case, the gathering is taking place today on a very large scale, as people from many lands are accepting the gospel and are gathering to the Lord's Church.

Some Old Testament Prophecies of Gathering

The Old Testament contains some beautiful prophecies concerning the gathering of Israel in the last days. One of the greatest prophecies concerning Israel's return to the covenants from its scattered and disbelieving state is found in Jeremiah 16:13–21. In this passage, the prophet foretold the marvelous future event that would eclipse in its greatness and glory the exodus from Egypt. In the splendor of this latter-day event, the mighty act of divine deliverance in Moses' day would no longer be remembered. The event that Jeremiah envisioned is the latter-day gathering of Israel, described as follows: "Behold, I will send for many fishers, saith the Lord, and they shall fish them; and after will I send for many hunters, and they shall hunt them from every mountain, and from every hill, and out of the holes of the rocks. For mine eyes are upon all their ways: they are not hid from my face" (Jer. 16:16–17). In the ancient prophet's inspired view, the hundreds of thousands of Latter-day Saints who have served missions are the fishers and hunters who have gathered to the covenants the scattered Israelites of whom Jeremiah wrote. Indeed, those Israelites are not lost from the Lord. The same scene of the latter-day return surpassing that of ancient times is found in Jeremiah 23:7–8. It follows a beautiful prophecy in which the Lord promises to gather his scattered people as a shepherd gathers his sheep. The Lord promises further that he would set up shepherds over those who return, who would care for them, feed them, and protect them (see Jer. 23:3–4). The greatest of the shepherds will be Israel's millennial king David, who is the Lord Jesus Christ (see Jer. 23:5–6; see chapter 11 in this volume).

Jeremiah foretold the establishment of God's new and everlasting covenant with Israel and Judah. "Behold, the days come, saith the Lord, that I will make a new covenant with the house of Israel, and with the house of Judah" (Jer. 31:31; see also vv. 32–33). The latter-day covenant would be different from the covenant made in the days of Moses. Whereas that covenant was written on tablets of stone, the covenant of which Jeremiah spoke would be written in people's hearts. So great would be their commitment to it that no one in that day would need to warn his neighbor, "saying, Know the Lord," for they would all know him, "from the least of them unto the greatest of them" (Jer. 31:33–34; see also 32:39–40). The new and everlasting covenant is the fulness of the gospel (see D&C 39:11; 66:2). It is "new" and "everlasting" in contrast to the "old" and "temporary" covenant of the law of Moses, to which Jeremiah compared it. It was established in the Church in Jesus' day, as it had been in the times of earlier righteous Saints prior to the days of Moses. We live now in the day when it has been reestablished with Israel; thus Jeremiah's prophecy has found partial fulfillment already. Its ultimate fulfillment will be in the Millennium, the period of time concerning which Jeremiah wrote, when Judah will join Israel in that covenant and all people will know the Lord.

Jeremiah also foretold Ephraim's role in the restoration of Israel:

"For there shall be a day, that the watchmen upon mount Ephraim shall cry, Arise ye, and let us go up to Zion unto the Lord our God" (Jer. 31:6). Of note is the fact that it would be Ephraim that would announce to his brethren of Israel that the time for their return had come. Jeremiah told of that return in a beautiful image of traveling in safety and peace: "They shall come with weeping, and with supplications, will I lead them: I will cause them to walk by the rivers of waters in a straight way, wherein they shall not stumble: for I am a father to Israel, and Ephraim is my firstborn" (Jer. 31:9).

The prophet Ezekiel also bore testimony of those great latter-day events, recording the Lord's words as follows: "Thus saith the Lord God; Behold, I will take the children of Israel from among the heathen, whither they be gone, and will gather them on every side, and bring them into their own land: And I will make them one nation in the land upon the mountains of Israel; and one king shall be king to them all: and they shall be no more two nations, neither shall they be divided into two kingdoms any more at all" (Ezek. 37:21–22). In that millennial day, Jesus himself, who is the heir to the throne of David and the one to whom kingship rightly belongs, will be the king of reunited Israel. He and his people will live in peace and happiness and will share in the blessings of the covenant: "So shall they be my people, and I will be their God. And David my servant shall be king over them; and they all shall have one shepherd: they shall also walk in my judgments, and observe my statutes, and do them. And they shall dwell in the land that I have given unto Jacob my servant, wherein your fathers have dwelt; and they shall dwell therein, even they, and their children, and their children's children for ever: and my servant David shall be their prince for ever. Moreover I will make a covenant of peace with them; it shall be an everlasting covenant with them: and I will place them, and multiply them, and will set my sanctuary in the midst of them for evermore. My tabernacle also shall be with them: yea, I will be their God, and they shall be my people" (Ezek. 37:23–27).

NOTES

1. See John Bright, *A History of Israel,* 3d ed. (Philadelphia, Westminster, 1972), 269–309.

2. See James B. Pritchard, ed., *Ancient Near Eastern Texts Relating to the Old Testament,* 3d ed. with supp. (Princeton, N.J.: Princeton University Press, 1969), 282–301.

3. See K. Lawson Younger Jr., "Israelites in Exile," *Biblical Archaeology Review* 29, no. 6 (November/December 2003), 36–45, 65–66.

4. A secondhand statement attributed to Joseph Smith, first attested in 1882, identifies Ishmael as a descendant of Ephraim. See *Journal of Discourses,* 26 vols. (Liverpool: Latter-day Saints' Book Depot, 1854–86), 23:184–85.

5. See Bright, *History of Israel,* 343–60. For a sample of inscriptional evidence for the presence of Jews in Babylonia in the sixth century and later, see Michael D. Coogan, *West Semitic Personal Names in the Murašû Documents,* Harvard Semitic Monograph 7 (Missoula, Mont: Harvard Semitic Museum/Scholars Press, 1976).

6. E.g., Jeremiah 23:3–4; 31:10; Ezekiel 34:2–24.

7. E.g., Isaiah 5:1–7; Jeremiah 2:21; 24:1–10; Matthew 3:9–10; 1 Nephi 10:12; Jacob 5.

8. E.g., Ezekiel 11:19–20; 36:26–27.

9. E.g., Isaiah 57:7–8; Jeremiah 3:6–20; Ezekiel 16:1–63; 23:1–49; Hosea 1:2–11; 2:1–3:3; Matthew 25:1–13; Revelation 19:6–9. See also Kent P. Jackson, "The Marriage of Hosea and Jehovah's Covenant with Israel," in Monte S. Nyman, ed., *Isaiah and the Prophets* (Provo, Utah: Religious Studies Center, Brigham Young University, 1984), 57–73.

10. E.g., Isaiah 11:10–13, 16; 19:23; 35:8; 49:22; Ezekiel 37:1–14; Doctrine and Covenants 113:6; 115:5–6; 133:25–27.

11. Andrew F. Ehat and Lyndon W. Cook, eds., *The Words of Joseph Smith: The Contemporary Accounts of the Nauvoo Discourses of the Prophet Joseph* (Provo, Utah: Religious Studies Center, Brigham Young University, 1980), 212; spelling standardized where necessary for readability.

12. Spencer W. Kimball, *The Teachings of Spencer W. Kimball,* ed. Edward L. Kimball (Salt Lake City: Bookcraft, 1982), 439.

5

The Gathering of Joseph, the Gentiles, and the Jews

The key tribe in the latter-day gathering of Israel is Ephraim, which has the calling of leadership in the house of Israel. It is significant to note that though the man Ephraim received the birthright with its keys of presidency in the days of his grandfather Jacob (see Gen. 48:10–22; 49:22–26), the tribe that bore his name never did preside over the combined tribes. Even in the days of Jacob the word of prophecy foretold that Judah would assume the leadership instead (see Gen. 49:8–10). That was realized in the kingship of David and his descendants, and its ultimate fulfillment will be in the millennial kingship of the Lord Jesus Christ. Though Ephraim was perhaps the most populous of the northern tribes, its calling to leadership over the twelve never was exercised in biblical times, nor was it ever until the nineteenth century after Christ, when the Lord began his preparations for the latter-day redemption of his covenant people.

The Gathering of Joseph

We have no scriptural record of Ephraim and the other northern tribes from Old Testament times until early in the nineteenth century after Christ when some of their number began to be identified in such places as New York, Ohio, and Europe—far from Halah, Habor, and the cities of the Medes to which the Bible tells us their ancestors were taken (see 2 Kgs. 17:6; D&C 86:8–11; 133:25–35). It is impossible to trace the history of the northern tribes of Israel from their deportation to Mesopotamia in the eighth century before Christ to the beginning of their latter-day gathering. Patriarchal blessings have identified the overwhelming majority of Latter-day Saints of European, Asian, and African ancestry as descendants of Ephraim, showing that during the course of history, the lineage of Ephraim spread throughout the earth. Although sensational and unattested accounts of Israel's wanderings have been popular in the Church for many years,[1] historians do see evidence of the movements of peoples over time. But even more significant than the wanderings of nations is the fact that over the centuries, the lineage of a small group of individuals or families can spread through a large population.

The key individual in the latter-day gathering of Israel is Joseph Smith (see chapter 10). God began his work in the last days by calling his great prophet of the tribe of Ephraim. Through him the fulness of the gospel was restored in new revelations, including the scriptural records of two branches of the house of Israel—the Book of Mormon and the Doctrine and Covenants. The gathering thus began with a restoration; indeed, without the Restoration there could be no gathering, for it is a gathering first and foremost to the gospel and to the covenants that pertain to it. Others of Ephraim were gathered through the testimony of Joseph Smith, and soon a nucleus of Ephraimites had entered into the covenants that God had made with their fathers. Since that nucleus was formed over a century and a half ago, many others have joined them in those covenants. Missionaries have been sent out since the beginning of the Church to gather more of their fellows of the house of Israel. Although we have Saints today whom patriarchs have identified as coming from all twelve of the Israelite tribes, the vast majority of those who have been gathered to the Church so far are of Ephraim. Ephraim has thus assumed its latter-day leadership role by being the first to gather to the gospel and return to the Lord's Church. And it is primarily Ephraim that gathers the other tribes. Ephraim has the keys and the ministry to take the gospel to his brethren and to bring them home again to the covenant family (see Jer. 31:6–7; D&C 133:26–32).

Many thousands of the descendants of Ephraim have been gathered again to the covenant family. We Latter-day Saints are so close to this marvelous process that we sometimes take it for granted, overlooking its significance and desiring to look beyond it for something that appears to be more sensational. But consider the miraculous nature of the gathering foretold in the scriptures that is taking place in the Church today: Many years ago, Israelites of the tribe of Ephraim, in an apostate condition, were taken by Assyrian kings and transported from their homeland to other parts of the Near East. Very soon they became lost from history, probably because they lost the knowledge of their own identity among the nations in which they were scattered. Following some 2,600 years outside the knowledge of the Jewish and Christian worlds, many of their descendants began to be recognized, identified, and gathered again to the gospel fold of their ancient Shepherd. It is not without reason that Jeremiah should proclaim that this latter-day gathering eclipses the magnitude of the gathering brought about under the direction of Moses (see Jer. 23:7–8). It is a miraculous event, even though greater aspects of it are yet to come.

Ephraim's brother-tribe Manasseh has been the second to rejoin the covenants. In 1828, almost two years before the Church was organized, the Prophet Joseph Smith was told of the latter-day conversion of Lehi's children and the role that the Book of Mormon would play in that process: "And for this very purpose are these plates preserved, which contain these records—that the promises of the Lord might be fulfilled, which he made to his people; and that the Lamanites might come to the knowledge of their fathers, and that they might know the promises of the Lord, and that they may believe the gospel and rely upon the merits of Jesus Christ, and be glorified through faith in his name, and that through their repentance, they might be saved" (D&C 3:19–20). Scarcely six months after the organization of the Church, the Lord announced the beginning of the gathering of Lehi's children (see D&C 28:8; 32:1–5). Many of the descendants of the Book of Mormon peoples are now members of the Lord's Church and have been identified in patriarchal blessings as children of Manasseh and Ephraim. They are joining the Church at the rate of many thousands per year. Manasseh has joined hands with Ephraim, and together they have done a great work in gathering others of their Josephite brethren into the blessings of the gospel. This is the day of the gathering of Manasseh and Ephraim, and it begins the day of the gathering of all of Israel (see 3 Ne. 21:1–7, 26–29).[2]

THE GATHERING OF THE GENTILES

The word *Gentile,* which is found often in the scriptures, requires clarification. In the Book of Mormon worldview, the human family of the latter days includes the children of Lehi, the Jews, the lost tribes (scattered among the nations), and the Gentiles. Because the scattered remnants of ancient Israel are located among the Gentiles, the Book of Mormon sometimes calls them Gentiles, and indeed they are Gentiles culturally (see 1 Ne. 15:13–14; 22:7–12). In the Old Testament the term is used differently. The Hebrew word *gôy* is a noun meaning "nation" or "people," used in reference to the nations of the world. In a theological sense, the Old Testament term *Gentiles,* as well as its synonyms *nations, stranger,* and *heathen,* refer to those who are not

Israel. I will use the term *Gentile* to refer to those who are not descendants of Israel, as it is used in the Bible.

The scriptures teach that in addition to Israelites accepting the gospel, Gentiles will do so as well (e.g., Jer. 16:19–21). Abraham was promised that many who are not his descendants but who accept the gospel would "be called after [his] name" and "be accounted [his] seed" and "rise up and bless [him], as their father" (Abr. 2:10). "There can be no misunderstanding of this statement," wrote Elder John A. Widtsoe. "All who accept the gospel become by adoption members of the family of Abraham."[3] Paul, the apostle to the Gentiles in the early Church (see Gal. 2:7–8), spoke of this happening in his own time: "For as many of you as have been baptized into Christ have put on Christ. There is neither Jew nor Greek [i.e., Gentile], . . . for ye are all one in Christ Jesus. And if ye be Christ's, then are ye Abraham's seed, and heirs according to the promise" (Gal. 3:27–29). Thus those non-Israelites who accept the gospel become heirs of all of the blessings promised to the Patriarchs and their descendants. They become inheritors of the covenants in their fullest degree, with all of the promises of those who are heirs by natural genealogical descent (see Isa. 56:6–8). As Nephi said, "As many of the Gentiles as will repent are the covenant people of the Lord" (2 Ne. 30:2). And as Jesus taught, "If the Gentiles will repent and return unto me, saith the Father, behold they shall be numbered among my people, O house of Israel" (3 Ne. 16:13). They become members of Israel, because Israel is the name of the covenant family, and those who enter the covenants become members of the family.

The New Testament gives additional information concerning the future conversion of Gentiles and the requirements for membership in the house of Israel. When confronted by self-righteous Pharisees boastful of their Abrahamic lineage, John the Baptist challenged them to do the works required of covenant people, or the covenant blessings would be taken from them and given to those who are not of Abraham's line: "Bring forth therefore fruits worthy of repentance, and begin not to say within yourselves, We have Abraham to our father: for I say unto you, That God is able of these stones to raise up children unto Abraham" (Luke 3:8). God can raise up covenant people from among the Gentiles, if the natural heirs to the covenants do not bring forth the good works required for the blessings. John continued, "And now also the axe is laid unto the root of the trees: every tree therefore which bringeth not forth good fruit is hewn down, and cast into the fire" (Luke 3:9). The tree of the house of Israel would be cut down, and its blessings would be given to others. Jesus' parable of the Great Supper also teaches this doctrine (see Luke 14:16–24). In it, as Elder James E. Talmage taught, "the covenant people, Israel, were the specially invited guests. They had been bidden long enough aforetime, and by their own profession as the Lord's own had agreed to be partakers of the feast."[4] Yet when the call to come was extended to them, they refused and offered weak excuses for their absence. "Then the gladsome invitation was to be carried to the Gentiles, who were looked upon as spiritually poor, maimed, halt, and blind. And later, even the pagans beyond the walls, strangers in the gates of the holy city, would be bidden to the supper."[5] The parable concludes with these words of the master whose feast it was: "None of those men which were bidden shall taste of my supper" (Luke 14:24).

As John the Baptist said, "Bring forth therefore fruits meet for repentance" (Matt. 3:8). That is what determines whether we are chosen people. And Gentile non-Israelites can do so and enjoy the covenant blessings. Paul stated, "For they are not all Israel, which are of Israel. Neither, because they are the seed of Abraham, are they all children" (Rom. 9:6–7). What matters is that one is spiritually reborn into the covenants by accepting the Lord's atoning grace, exercising faith, repentance, and righteous works. In this day of the gathering of Joseph, it is not unlikely that the gathering of righteous non-Israelites is also taking place. They are brought into the house of Israel and receive their birthright in one of the tribes under the inspired hands of a patriarch. We make no distinction among ourselves between those who are the natural branches and those who are grafted into the house of Israel through adoption. All are "Abraham's seed, and heirs according to the promise" (Gal. 3:29). And "all are alike unto God" (2 Ne. 26:33).

THE GATHERING OF THE JEWS

Most of the Old Testament prophecies of gathering deal with the house of Israel as a whole, and perhaps even more specifically with the scattered tribes of the northern kingdom. The scriptures suggest that Judah's return, except in isolated cases, will take a different form than that of his brethren. Elder Bruce R. McConkie wrote: "As all the world knows, many Jews are now gathering to Palestine, where they have their own nation and way of worship, all without reference to a belief in Christ or an acceptance of the laws and ordinances of his everlasting gospel. Is this the latter-day gathering of the Jews of which the scriptures speak? No! It is not; let there be no misunderstanding in any discerning mind on this point. This gathering of the Jews to their homeland, and their organization into a nation and a kingdom, is not the gathering promised by the prophets. It does not fulfill the ancient promises."[6]

What are those ancient promises to which Elder McConkie referred? The Book of Mormon prophet Jacob taught of the future of the Jews from his own day into a distant time (see 2 Ne. 6:8–11). In his revelation he told that they would be scattered, but one day they would return: "When they shall come to the knowledge of their Redeemer, they shall be gathered together again to the lands of their inheritance" (2 Ne. 6:11). His brother Nephi bore a similar testimony of Judah's return: "When that day cometh, saith the prophet, that they no more turn aside their hearts against the Holy One of Israel, then will he remember the covenants which he made to their fathers. Yea, then will he remember the isles of the sea; yea, and all the people who are of the house of Israel, will I gather in, saith the Lord . . . from the four quarters of the earth" (1 Ne. 19:15–16; see also 3 Ne. 5:25–26). A millennial setting for the fulfillment of this prophecy is suggested in the statement that all scattered Israelites would be gathered in that day (see 1 Ne. 19:16; cf. D&C 133:25–35) and that "all the earth" would "see the salvation of the Lord" (1 Ne. 19:17). The resurrected Savior testified to the Nephites and Lamanites of those same truths concerning their brethren the Jews and their return to their promised land: "And it shall come to pass that the time cometh, when the fulness of my gospel shall be preached unto them; and they shall believe in me, that I am Jesus Christ, the Son of God, and shall pray unto the father in my name. Then shall their watchmen lift up their voice, and with the voice together shall they sing; for they shall see eye to eye. Then will the Father gather them together again, and give unto them Jerusalem for the land of their inheritance" (3 Ne. 20:30–33). The verses that follow in the Savior's discourse to the Nephites make it clear that he is describing millennial events.

These Book of Mormon passages thus set forth the following sequence for the gathering of the Jews: (1) the gospel will be preached to them; (2) they will be converted to it and join the Church of Jesus Christ; and (3) then the Lord will gather them to their ancient homeland. The gathering of the branches of Israel is first to the gospel and the Church and then later to promised lands, because an inheritance in a promised land is a blessing of the covenant, and it is only in the covenant that the blessing can be obtained.

On 24 October 1841, Elder Orson Hyde, holding the holy apostleship and acting under the direction of the Prophet Joseph Smith, dedicated the land of Palestine for the return of the Jews, the building up of Jerusalem, and the construction of a temple there. He implored the Father to "restore the kingdom unto Israel—raise up Jerusalem as its capital, and constitute her people a distinct nation and government, with David thy servant, even a descendant from the loins of ancient David, to be their king."[7] Latter-day Saints look forward to that day, which the Book of Mormon places in a millennial setting, as does the Old Testament. The rebuilt Jerusalem that Elder Hyde's dedication promised will be constructed by the Lord's millennial disciples, for the Jerusalem that now stands, according to the Book of Mormon, must "pass away" and "become new" (Ether 13:9). The people who will inhabit the Holy City when the millennial King will rule will be those, according to Ether, who "have been washed in the blood of the Lamb; and they are they who were scattered and gathered in from the four quarters of the earth, and from the north countries, and are partakers of the fulfilling of the covenant which God made with their father, Abraham" (Ether 13:11).

On 2 August 1831, Elder Sidney Rigdon, acting under the direction of and in the presence of the Prophet Joseph Smith, dedicated the land of Zion in western Missouri "for a possession and inheritance for the Saints. . . . and for all the faithful servants of the Lord to the remotest ages of time."[8] The next day the Prophet himself dedicated a site for the temple.[9] Church members flocked to Missouri to take possession of their prophesied inheritance. But history records that their dreams were not realized, for receiving an inheritance in a promised land is conditioned upon living the law that the Lord has established for that land, and the Saints were not yet ready.

The circumstances at the location of the future New Jerusalem parallel those at the site of Old Jerusalem. As our brothers and sisters of Judah embrace their Savior Jesus Christ, the Lord will gather and establish them in the land of their fathers. The timing of these events is not always clear in the scriptures, but it appears that much or most of this will take place in the Millennium. The Doctrine and Covenants foretells: "And then shall the Lord set his foot upon this mount [the Mount of Olives in Jerusalem], and it shall cleave in twain, and the earth shall tremble, and reel to and fro, and the heavens also shall shake. . . . And then shall the Jews look upon me and say: What are these wounds in thine hands and in thy feet? Then shall they know that I am the Lord; for I will say unto them: These wounds are the wounds with which I was wounded in the house of my friends. I am he who was lifted up. I am Jesus that was crucified. I am the Son of God. And then shall they weep because of their iniquities; then shall they lament because they persecuted their king" (D&C 45:48, 51–53). The participants in this event of the Second Coming will perhaps be descendants of some who live in the Holy Land today. Only a small group in Jerusalem will be necessary to fulfill the prophecy, yet it applies to descendants of Judah everywhere, because they too will witness Jesus' return. Because this account probably symbolizes what will take place in the hearts of millions worldwide, perhaps those Jews present at Christ's coming on the Mount of Olives will already be Latter-day Saints (see D&C 45:43–44).

Jesus' coming will initiate an enormous process of conversion. Important things will need to follow, including teaching, baptizing, giving the gift of the Holy Ghost, organizing stakes and wards, and administering temple ordinances—all under the hands of priesthood authority. After the coming of the Savior, Latter-day Saint missionaries and priesthood leaders will teach the gospel to the scattered children of Israel all over the world. They will make known to them the covenants that God made with their fathers in ancient times, and they will bring them into the Lord's Church. Then will follow the physical gathering and restoration to Israel's lands of promise (see D&C 133:25–35). The Book of Mormon prophet Jacob foresaw that day and recorded Jesus' words: "But behold, thus saith the Lord God: When the day cometh that they shall believe in me, that I am Christ, then have I covenanted with their fathers that they shall be restored in the flesh, upon the earth, unto the lands of their inheritance. And it shall come to pass that they shall be gathered in from their long dispersion, from the isles of the sea, and from the four parts of the earth" (2 Ne. 10:7–8).

"Sanctified in Holiness before the Lord"

The gospel of Jesus Christ includes covenants that God makes with his children if they will accept them. Through ancient prophets and Patriarchs, the Lord has promised great blessings to all the branches of the house of Israel and to those Gentiles who join with the covenant family. But those promises are based on obedience to the commandments and cannot be received except on the condition of worthiness. "Behold, the Lord esteemeth all flesh in one; he that is righteous is favored of God" (1 Ne. 17:35). The latter days are the days of restoration, in which the Lord has restored to his Church the keys of the gathering of his children and will yet restore them into a nation of covenant people. As he said to the Prophet Joseph Smith concerning the happy state of the faithful, "And they shall be filled with songs of everlasting joy. Behold, this is the blessing of the everlasting God upon the tribes of Israel, and the richer blessing upon the head of Ephraim and his fellows. And they also of the tribe of Judah, after their pain, shall be sanctified in holiness before the Lord, to dwell in his presence day and night, forever and ever" (D&C 133:33–35).

Notes

1. A collection is found in E. L. Whitehead, *The House of Israel* (Salt Lake City: E. L. Whitehead, 1947).

2. See Kent P. Jackson, *The Restored Gospel and the Book of Genesis* (Salt Lake City: Deseret Book, 2001), 159–67.

3. John A. Widtsoe, *Evidences and Reconciliations,* arr. G. Homer Durham (Salt Lake City: Bookcraft, 1960), 399.

4. James E. Talmage, *Jesus the Christ* (Salt Lake City: Deseret Book, 1915), 452.

5. Talmage, *Jesus the Christ,* 452.

6. Bruce R. McConkie, *The Millennial Messiah* (Salt Lake City: Deseret Book, 1982), 229.

7. *Times and Seasons* 3, no. 11 (1 April 1842): 740.

8. "The Book of John Whitmer," 32, in Bruce N. Westergren, ed., *From Historian to Dissident: The Book of John Whitmer* (Salt Lake City: Signature, 1995), 86; spelling and capitalization standardized where necessary for readability.

9. Dean C. Jessee, ed., *The Papers of Joseph Smith: Vol. 1, Autobiographical and Historical Writings* (Salt Lake City: Deseret Book, 1989), 358, 360–61.

6

WHERE ARE THE "LOST TEN TRIBES"?

O ne of the most frequently asked doctrinal questions since the early days of the Church concerns the history and whereabouts of the Israelites sometimes called the "lost ten tribes." Yet "Where are the lost ten tribes?" is not a Latter-day Saint question at all. It was brought into the Church by early converts from other denominations, who were already speculating concerning it. It was asked more commonly in past generations, but even today the question still arises. It is unfortunate that it should be asked at all, however, because latter-day revelation gives clear teaching on the subject—as does the Bible. The expression "lost tribes" is found in only two verses of scripture—both in the Book of Mormon (see 2 Ne. 29:13; 3 Ne. 17:4). Both passages refer to members of the house of Israel outside their ancestral homeland. Nephi indicates that the word *lost* shows the perspective of the Israelites in Palestine: the "lost" tribes were simply "lost from the knowledge of those who are at Jerusalem" (1 Ne. 22:4). Thus those people are Israelites who were removed from Palestine and whose history was unknown to those who remained, including to the writers of the Bible and the Book of Mormon.

In the eighth century before Christ, the kingdom of Israel, consisting of the northern ten tribes, was destroyed because of the wickedness of its people. Many of its inhabitants were deported from their homeland by Assyrian conquerors and relocated in other places (see 2 Kgs. 15:29; 17:3–6, 23), where they became lost from the view of the rest of Israel. They and their descendants are the "lost tribes" because their identity was not known to the world and in most cases not even to themselves. When the term is used for the descendants of the deported northern tribes, it is synonymous with "ten tribes," an expression found only in Doctrine and Covenants 110:11 and Article of Faith 10.[1]

While there is much about the history of the lost tribes of Israel that is not known, they are not really lost. The scriptures tell us where they went, where they are today, and how they will return. Old Testament and Book of Mormon prophecies constitute our best source of information regarding their current whereabouts. The message is clear: They would be scattered among the nations of the earth. That is where they are today, and it is from that scattered condition that they are gathered again in the last days.

Moses prophesied: "The Lord shall scatter you among the nations, and ye shall be left few in number among the heathen, whither the Lord shall lead you" (Deut. 4:27). In that scattered state, the Israelites would no longer worship the Lord but would adopt the religions of the lands in which they would live (see Deut. 4:28), suggesting that they would also lose the knowledge of their Israelite heritage. Moses said: "The Lord shall scatter thee among all people, from the one end of the earth even unto the other; and there thou shalt serve other gods, which neither thou nor thy fathers have known, even wood and stone" (Deut. 28:64; see also Lev. 26:33). Hosea prophesied that the exiled Israelites would be "wanderers among the nations" (Hosea 9:17), and Amos said that the Lord would "sift" them "among all nations" (Amos 9:9). Years later, after Israel had been deported, the Lord told Ezekiel: "I lifted up mine hand unto them also in the wilderness, that I would scatter them among the heathen, and disperse them through the countries" (Ezek. 20:23). It should be noted that the words *Gentiles, nations, people,* and *heathen* in the King James Version are synonymous terms. They are all translated from the Hebrew words ʿammîm and gôyîm, both of which mean "nations" or "peoples" and refer to the non-Israelite nations of the world.

Book of Mormon prophecies are even more explicit about the lost tribes being scattered among the nations of the earth. Nephi taught: "The house of Israel, sooner or later, will be scattered upon all the face of the earth, and also among all nations" (1 Ne. 22:3). He continued, "And behold, there are many who are already lost from the knowledge of those who are at Jerusalem. Yea, the more part of all the tribes have been led away; and they are scattered to and fro" (1 Ne. 22:4).

Where will they be when the gathering takes place? Nephi taught that "after all the house of Israel have been scattered and confounded" (1 Ne. 22:7), the Lord would begin the process by which the covenants of the gospel would be brought to them, and they would be gathered again (see 1 Ne. 22:7–11). Thus they would still be in their scattered state throughout the world when the gospel would be brought to them by the Lord's missionaries. The Savior himself provided this explanation: "And then shall the remnants, which shall be scattered abroad upon the face of the earth, be gathered in from the east and from the west, and from the south and from the north; and they shall be brought to the knowledge of the Lord their God, who hath redeemed them" (3 Ne. 20:13; see also 21:26–29). The emphasis in these passages is clear: The Israelites would be scattered among the nations, and they would remain scattered until their latter-day gathering. Of course, these scriptures rule out the imaginative speculations that were once common in the Church—that the lost tribes are away from the earth, under the polar icecap, on the moon, and so forth.[2]

SOME UNANSWERED QUESTIONS

Where then did Jesus go after his stay with the Nephites and Lamanites in the land of Bountiful? When he taught them he said, "I have other sheep, which are not of this land, neither of the land of Jerusalem, neither in any parts of that land round about whither I have been to minister. For they of whom I speak are they who have not as yet heard my voice; neither have I at any time manifested myself unto them. But I have received a commandment of the Father that I shall go unto them, and that they shall hear my voice, and shall be numbered among my sheep, that there may be one fold and one shepherd; therefore I go to show myself unto them" (3 Ne. 16:1–3). Because Jesus called these people "other tribes whom [the Jews in Jerusalem] know not of" (3 Ne. 16:4), and because he was going to visit them personally (see 3 Ne. 15:23 and Matt. 15:24), we know that he was speaking of remnants of Israel (see especially 3 Ne. 17:4). If they were descendants of Israelites who had been deported by the Assyrians, we have no way of knowing where they were when he visited them. The northern tribes were in a state of apostasy when they were carried away, and their paganization was the reason why the Lord rejected them and drove them out of the land (see 2 Kgs. 17:7–23).

In the apocryphal book 2 Esdras (see 13:40–47), there is a fanciful account of a northward escape of the ten tribes from Assyria shortly after their exile began. The story, repeated from time to time in Latter-day Saint literature, dates from eight hundred years after the presumed event and is in a late, nonscriptural book that abounds in other material that is thoroughly unbelievable. There is no reason to accept any part of the story as history.

But if those whom Jesus visited were descendants of the northern tribes of Israel, as we assume they were, then certainly something must have happened to them to prepare them for

Jesus' coming. Perhaps after years of apostasy in the lands to which they had been taken, the Lord raised up prophets among them who restored some of them to their ancestral faith, preparing them for the visit of the Savior. Or perhaps the Lord raised up a prophet out of the scattered remnants of Israel and sent him and his family to a distant part of the earth, where they grew into a nation and were favored later with the Lord's visit. That would be similar to the means by which the Lord established a branch of Joseph in America, through the calling of Lehi and his family. If Lehi's experience is one of the patterns by which the Lord scattered Israel, then perhaps a prophet was called shortly before the destruction of Samaria, over a century before Jerusalem's fall, to take his family and journey to a new land. Perhaps that pattern was repeated on several occasions, with the Lord scattering parts of Israel by calling families to different parts of the earth. Perhaps it was to such a group or groups that the Lord came.[3]

We do not know if Jesus visited one group of Israelites or many after being with the children of Lehi. He stated simply, "I have other sheep" (3 Ne. 16:1), and "I go . . . to show myself unto the lost tribes of Israel, for they are not lost unto the Father, for he knoweth whither he hath taken them" (3 Ne. 17:4). While Jesus was among Lehi's descendants in America, he emphasized their responsibility to record his words so they would come forth in a later day (see 3 Ne. 23:4). Certainly he would have given a similar charge to others whom he visited (see 2 Ne. 29:11). When the time is right, those records too will be revealed and will become one with the records of Joseph and Judah. As the Lord revealed to Nephi, "For behold, I shall speak unto the Jews and they shall write it; and I shall also speak unto the Nephites and they shall write it; and I shall also speak unto the other tribes of the house of Israel, which I have led away, and they shall write it; and I shall also speak unto all nations of the earth and they shall write it. And it shall come to pass that the Jews shall have the words of the

Nephites, and the Nephites shall have the words of the Jews; and the Nephites and the Jews shall have the words of the lost tribes of Israel; and the lost tribes of Israel shall have the words of the Nephites and the Jews. And it shall come to pass that my people, which are of the house of Israel, shall be gathered home unto the lands of their possessions; and my word also shall be gathered in one" (2 Ne. 29:12–14).

Although some Latter-day Saints have spoken of lost tribes "bringing their records with them" when they return, no scripture foretells such an event. Lehi's descendants, a group that was lost from the view of the rest of Israel, wrote a sacred record of God's dealings with their prophets. Yet their record was not restored to the world through them. They were in a condition of spiritual darkness when it was brought forth and needed it to assist them in their own gathering. Their record was restored through the Prophet Joseph Smith, who held "the keys of the gathering of Israel from the four parts of the earth" (D&C 110:11). It is likely that other sacred records will be brought forth in the same manner, under the direction of the president of the Lord's Church, whether before or after the beginning of the Millennium.[4]

Another important clue concerning the history and whereabouts of the ten tribes creates an intriguing question. According to John Whitmer, early in June 1831 "the spirit of the Lord fell upon Joseph [Smith] in an unusual manner. And prophesied that John the Revelator was then among the ten tribes of Israel . . . to prepare them for their return, from their long dispersion."[5] This statement is consistent with John's mission as described in the Doctrine and Covenants "to gather the tribes of Israel" (D&C 77:14). But where were the ten tribes when John was among them in 1831? Were they in a group then? Not necessarily. Perhaps John's ministry to them took him into many lands. Did they know who he was, and did they know he was ministering to them? Not necessarily (see 3 Ne. 28:6, 27–28). Perhaps his ministry among them was that of a forerunner, to prepare them to receive the gospel message when it would be preached to them later. The scriptures call John an "Elias"—a forerunner (see D&C 77:14). Perhaps he ministered to them without revealing his true identity as an apostle of Christ (see Heb. 13:2). Perhaps many of those to whom he ministered have been gathered since he was among them in 1831. Since 1837, when missionary work first began outside North America, millions of individuals identified as members of lost tribes have been gathered to the Church. The accounts of the conversion of large groups of people in Europe during the nineteenth century and in Africa, Asia, and elsewhere during the twentieth century demonstrate that many scattered Israelites had been prepared beforehand "for their return, from their long dispersion." Perhaps John had been among them, and perhaps he is now performing similar service elsewhere in preparation for the time when doors will be opened in other parts of the earth for the return of others of Israel.

It is not unreasonable to suggest that others whom Jesus visited had a history similar to that of the family of Lehi. Jesus visited a group, or groups, just as he had done earlier at Bountiful, yet we do not know how they became a group—whether they left Palestine or Mesopotamia together or were gathered in a later century.[6] But we can conclude that those to whom he appeared were believers who, like Lehi's children, had been prepared in advance for his coming. Are those "lost tribes" still a group of believers today? Undoubtedly not. The scriptures emphasize their dispersion. Those whom Jesus visited probably became scattered after his stay among them, just as Lehi's children did. Because the scriptures teach that they are brought back to the covenants from a scattered condition in the last days (see 1 Ne. 22:7–11; 3 Ne. 20:13; 21:26–29), it is clear that they do not have the gospel among them until they are taught it by the Lord's servants, the missionaries of The Church of Jesus Christ of Latter-day Saints.

THE RETURN OF WHAT WAS LOST

The keys of the gathering of the lost tribes have been restored as part of the restoration of the gospel, and thus the gathering takes place under the direction of the leaders of the Church. On 3 April 1836, the ancient prophet Moses appeared to Joseph Smith in the Kirtland Temple and committed to him and the Church "the keys of the gathering of Israel from the four parts of the earth, and the leading of the ten tribes from the land of the north" (D&C 110:11). Because those who were deported by Assyria were taken northward, "the north" became a scriptural image for their departure and return. "Go and proclaim these words toward the north, and say, Return, thou backsliding Israel, saith the Lord" (Jer. 3:12); "The Lord liveth, that brought up the children of Israel from the land of the north, and from all the lands whither he had driven them" (Jer. 16:15); "Ho, ho, come forth, and flee from the land of the north, saith the Lord: for I have spread you abroad as the four winds of the heaven" (Zech. 2:6). In modern revelation, the image continues in striking language: "And they who are in the north countries shall come in remembrance before the Lord; and their prophets shall hear his voice, and shall no longer stay themselves; and they shall smite the rocks, and the ice shall flow down at their presence" (D&C 133:26). Just as he did to bring the ancient Israelites out of Egypt, the Lord will prepare a way—a "highway"—to bring modern Israel home to promised covenants and promised lands (D&C 133:27; see Isa. 11:16; 35:8–10). Under the keys of the gathering, scattered Israelites will return from their places of dispersion: "And then shall the remnants, which shall be scattered abroad upon the face of the earth, be gathered in from the east and from the west, and from the south and from the north" (3 Ne. 20:13; see also Isa. 43:5–6). As they gather, they will forsake the old enmities that once separated the branches of Israel (see 2 Ne. 21:12–13), and each branch will possess the sacred records of the other (see 2 Ne. 29:11–14).

It should be clear that descendants of the lost tribes are gathering now. Ephraim is one of the lost ten tribes, and so is Manasseh, and the name Ephraim is used sometimes in the Bible as a name for *all* of the ten tribes (see Isa. 7:2–17; 11:13; Hosea 5:3–14). Ephraimites and others of Israel are gathering in large numbers now, as they embrace the message of the gospel taught them by the missionaries, join the Church, accept the covenants and ordinances, receive patriarchal blessings, and thus regain their identity as members of the house of Israel. The lost tribe of Ephraim has a book of modern scripture, the Doctrine and Covenants, and believing descendants of Judah, Lehi, and the lost tribes now each possess sacred records of the others, though more is yet to be revealed (see 2 Ne. 29:12–13). For all three groups, however, the Book of Mormon is a key to their conversion and thus also to their gathering (see Title Page; 3 Ne. 16:4–5).

The vast majority of Church members today are gathered descendants of the lost tribes of Israel and can see in themselves the fulfillment of ancient promises. But despite the Church's impressive growth now, the gathering is far from complete. A greater gathering, and the final return and restoration of all who were once lost, will be in the Millennium (see 2 Ne. 29:11–14; 3 Ne. 21:25–29).

NOTES

1. These were not the only Israelites to become "lost." Lehi and his group became lost from the knowledge of those who remained when the Lord led them away to a new land. Their descendants remain lost except to those who believe in the Book of Mormon, who recognize the Israelite heritage of the indigenous peoples of the Americas. The Jews were taken into

exile and eventually were scattered into many parts of the world. Yet many of them are not lost, because they have retained a knowledge of who they are.

2. An additional evidence is found in the New Testament. James addressed his general epistle "to the twelve tribes which are scattered abroad" (James 1:1). While undoubtedly referring to the scattered early Christian Church, James's greeting nonetheless emphasizes the concept of the tribes of Israel being scattered.

3. The Book of Mormon offers an additional possibility for some of the Israelites whom the Lord visited after his stay with the believers in the land of Bountiful. Book of Mormon passages speak of vast migrations of people from Zarahemla and Bountiful to "the land northward" and elsewhere, from which they never returned (see Alma 63:4–9; cf. Hel. 3:10–12). Those migrations happened within a century prior to the Lord's appearance to the Saints at Bountiful, and those who migrated were lost forever from the knowledge of the Nephites. Mormon wrote, "They were never heard of more," and where they went "we know not" (Alma 63:8). Perhaps they were among those whom Jesus visited.

4. See Bruce R. McConkie, *The Millennial Messiah* (Salt Lake City: Deseret Book, 1982), 217.

5. "The Book of John Whitmer," 27, in Bruce N. Westergren, ed., *From Historian to Dissident: The Book of John Whitmer* (Salt Lake City: Signature, 1995), 69–70; capitalization standardized where necessary for readability.

6. See McConkie, *Millennial Messiah*, 216–17. Elder McConkie presents a compelling case that the histories of the other groups Jesus visited are probably quite similar to the history of Lehi's descendants.

7

WHO WROTE ISAIAH?

The book of Isaiah has been the subject of intense study by Bible scholars for the past two centuries. As could be predicted, a variety of biases and approaches has yielded a variety of conclusions. One common interpretation among critical scholars is that the book in its present state is not the product of one author but of two, three, or perhaps more.[1] Given the world view of its proponents, this multiple-authorship proposal is inevitable. But the principal presupposition upon which it is based is clearly false, and for Latter-day Saints the Book of Mormon provides strong evidence in behalf of the essential unity of the book as we have it.

Although several different approaches to dividing Isaiah have been put forward, the following is the most common system:

First Isaiah—chapters 1–39: From Isaiah son of Amoz, ca. 740–700 B.C. (chapters 1–35); plus an extended excerpt from 2 Kings (chapters 36–39).

Second Isaiah—chapters 40–55: From an anonymous prophet (often called Deutero-Isaiah) during the Babylonian exile, ca. 540 B.C.[2]

Third Isaiah—chapters 56–66: From one or more anonymous disciples of Second Isaiah after the return from exile, ca. 515 B.C. Some commentators include these chapters under Deutero-Isaiah.

According to the proponents of multiple authorship, the

anonymous Second and Third Isaiah materials became attached to Isaiah's writings probably because the succeeding prophets were disciples of the first and the entire collection was viewed as representing one specific branch of prophetic tradition. Scholars who hold to the theory generally do so for the following major reasons:

1. Unlike First Isaiah, the prophecies in Second and Third Isaiah make no mention of Isaiah's name and give no other biographical clues that would link them to him.

2. The historical setting of Second and Third Isaiah is different from that of First Isaiah, as in the following examples: (a) Cyrus, a Persian king who lived over a century after Isaiah, is mentioned by name; (b) emphasis is placed on the power of the Babylonians, who in Isaiah's day were neither powerful nor very important politically; (c) the cities of Judah are already described as being destroyed, seemingly reflecting circumstances a century after Isaiah; (d) the temple is described as already being in ruins, though it was not destroyed until 586 B.C.; and (e) the Israelites are described as already being punished and exiled, which took place after 586 B.C.

3. The theological perspective is different: There is a shift from judgment to reconciliation. While the theme of God's coming judgment is indeed found in the last half of the book, it does not receive the emphasis there that it does in chapters 1–35. Similarly, though forgiveness and reconciliation are found in First Isaiah, in chapters 40–66 they predominate.

4. The literary style of chapters 40–66 differs from that of the earlier chapters.

These are interesting observations, and for the most part they accurately represent the change in tone that begins in chapter 40. But by no means do they constitute grounds for denying the material in chapters 40–66 to Isaiah son of Amoz.

PROPHETIC FORESIGHT

The fundamental issue in the multiple-authorship theory is whether a prophet can see beyond his own time. Those who begin with the presupposition that men cannot see beyond their own day must logically conclude that Isaiah could not have written those sections of the book that speak to a different historical setting than his own. But those who understand the true nature of revelation and prophetic foresight have no trouble with prophecies of future events. Latter-day Saints are blessed with abundant evidence revealed in the latter days that shows that God can indeed inspire his servants with views of future days, and when appropriate they impart that vision to others.

Some responses to the question of authorship include the following:

1. While it is true that Isaiah's name is never mentioned after chapter 39, neither do the later chapters ascribe authorship to anyone else. The earliest-known translation of Isaiah (the Greek Septuagint, third century before Christ) and the earliest existing manuscript of Isaiah (1QIs^a, the Isaiah Scroll from Qumran, second century before Christ) both include all the material now found in the book of Isaiah. No ancient document—including the New Testament and the rabbinic literature—shows any hint that readers in antiquity questioned Isaiah's authorship of the entire book.[3] The fact that the material is found in the book of Isaiah—and has been as far back as the evidence can be traced—clearly places the burden of proof on those who choose to assign it to other authors.

2. The material in chapters 40–66 does seem to address, to a degree, historical circumstances different from those of Isaiah's day. In the Book of Mormon we find a similar situation. President Ezra Taft Benson reminded the Church in 1986 that the Book of Mormon "was written for our day,"[4] adding his witness on that topic to those expressed by the book's authors. Moroni explained:

"Behold, I speak unto you as if ye were present, and yet ye are not. But behold, Jesus Christ hath shown you unto me, and I know your doing" (Morm. 8:35). As the Nephite writers saw and understood our time, they also wrote to meet our needs, not exclusively those of their contemporaries, who would never see the Book of Mormon as we have it. In the book of Isaiah is a striking parallel: Isaiah saw and understood the circumstances of his countrymen a century and one-half after his death, and through the inspiration of heaven he wrote in their behalf, as he also did for his contemporaries. But his scope does not stop there. He also saw our own latter-day setting, and the powerful witness that he left in his record speaks to our generation as well, when appropriately "likened" unto us (see 1 Ne. 19:23).

3. A significant shift in tone and subject matter does begin in chapter 40, and the shift was deliberate. In the prophetic books of the Old Testament, generally prophecies of judgment and punishment precede those of blessing and restoration. This is as true within individual prophecies and chapters as it is in the organization of entire books. This order of things mirrors real life, particularly the history of the house of Israel: God's judgment would be the inevitable consequence of Israel's rebellion; but in the latter days Israel would repent, be gathered and restored, and enjoy full reconciliation with its God. It seems likely that Isaiah's prophecies were meant to follow the same sequence. We should not be surprised if he prepared two collections of revelations (or if his followers arranged them later)—one, chapters 1–39, a "Book of Judgment," and the other, chapters 40–66, a "Book of Reconciliation."[5]

4. Even conservative scholars who argue for the unity of the entire book note stylistic differences between First and Second (and Third) Isaiah. More significant, however, is that even critical scholars who argue for multiple authorship see a great deal of Isaiah son of Amoz throughout the entire collection, pointing to "Isaianic" themes carried on by Deutero-Isaiah and his

successors.[6] It is important to note that almost all of Isaiah is written in poetry, and Hebrew poetry has sufficient flexibility to allow an author a wide range of literary options. Thus arguments for different literary styles are inconclusive, especially since we do not know the history of Isaiah's words once they left his mouth or his pen.

5. Those who believe in the Book of Mormon have additional evidence for the essential unity of the book of Isaiah, at least through chapter 55. When Lehi and his family left Jerusalem, they took with them the plates of brass, which contained, among other things, the writings of Isaiah, who predated Lehi by about one hundred years. The Nephite authors quoted extensively from Isaiah and included all or parts of the following chapters of Isaiah in the Book of Mormon: 2–14, 28–29, 40, 48–55.[7] The Book of Mormon thus proves that at least those chapters were known to be the writings of Isaiah when Lehi left Jerusalem in 600 B.C.—many decades before Second and Third Isaiah were supposed to have been written.[8] This is the most important piece of evidence for Isaiah's authorship of later chapters.

AN ANTHOLOGY OF PROPHETIC THOUGHT

Latter-day Saints, who accept the evidence from the Book of Mormon and believe that prophets can write to future generations, should have no difficulty accepting the essential unity of the book of Isaiah as the product of Isaiah son of Amoz from the eighth century before Christ. Yet many interesting questions remain to be answered. The great Old Testament scholar W. F. Albright pointed out that the prophetic books are not books but "anthologies of oracles and sermons."[9] This description certainly fits the book of Isaiah. Like the Bible itself, it is not a book, but a collection. And, like the Bible itself, the circumstances under which it was written and compiled are not clearly known. Did Isaiah record his prophecies himself, or did he dictate them to scribes? If they were dictated, was Isaiah responsible for their final poetic structure, or were others? Did Isaiah gather and compile the revelations himself, or did others do it? Were they collected in his lifetime, or later? Were they edited or reworded by later scribes?[10]

Though the answers to these questions are not critical for our understanding of Isaiah's message, they may explain such things as changes in emphasis, organization, and literary style of the revelations that make up the book of Isaiah.

NOTES

1. Good summaries are provided in W. S. LaSor, D. A. Hubbard, and F. W. Bush, *Old Testament Survey* (Grand Rapids, Mich.: Eerdmans, 1982), 371–77; R. K. Harrison, *Introduction to the Old Testament* (Grand Rapids, Mich.: Eerdmans, 1969), 764–80; B. W. Anderson, *Understanding the Old Testament,* 4th ed. (Englewood Cliffs, N.J.: Prentice-Hall, 1986), 321–23, 472–75, 502–6.

2. Anderson assigns chapters 34–35 to Deutero-Isaiah also; *Understanding the Old Testament,* 322.

3. The earliest known suggestion of multiple authorship comes from Rabbi Ibn-Ezra in the twelfth century after Christ.

4. Benson, Conference Report, October 1986, 5.

5. Chapters 36–39, excerpted from 2 Kings 18:13–20:19, provide a bridge between the "Book of Judgment" and the "Book of Reconciliation." The book of Ezekiel similarly contains an unmistakable shift in tone that begins after the prophet learned that Jerusalem had fallen (Ezek. 33:21). The earlier part of the book is a message of doom for Judah and other nations. The latter part is, for the most part, a message of future hope.

6. E.g., Anderson, *Understanding the Old Testament,* 504–6.

7. Monte S. Nyman, *"Great Are the Words of Isaiah"* (Salt Lake City: Bookcraft, 1980), 283–87.

8. Since nothing from Third Isaiah is contained in the Nephite record, the Book of Mormon argument cannot be used to prove Isaiah's authorship of chapters 56–66.

9. William F. Albright, *From the Stone Age to Christianity,* 2d ed. (Garden City, N.Y.: Doubleday/Anchor, 1957), 275.

10. A rabbinic tradition (*Baba Bathra* 15a) states that the book was compiled by "Hezekiah and his company." Hezekiah was the king of Judah during a significant portion of Isaiah's ministry.

8

HOW TO READ ISAIAH

In the record of their ministries contained in the Book of Mormon, Nephi and Jacob included eighteen chapters from Isaiah's writings as found on the plates of brass.[1] Nephi wrote: "I do not write anything upon plates save it be that I think it be sacred" (1 Ne. 19:6). Even though space on the plates was limited, they felt that Isaiah's message was important enough for their descendants and the Gentiles of the latter days that they should quote whole sections of it. Nephi's reasons for doing so are clear: "That I might more fully persuade them to believe in the Lord their Redeemer I did read unto them that which was written by the prophet Isaiah" (1 Ne. 19:23). "My soul delighteth in his words," he wrote, "for he verily saw my Redeemer, even as I have seen him" (2 Ne. 11:2; see also 25:5).[2] Nephi's love for Isaiah's words is a blessing for us. In his record in the Book of Mormon, he discusses how to read Isaiah, and he models the process.

Jacob explained why Isaiah's words had special value for his people: They concerned "all the house of Israel; wherefore, they may be likened unto you, for ye are of the house of Israel. And there are many things which have been spoken by Isaiah which may be likened unto you, because ye are of the house of Israel" (2 Ne. 6:5). Nephi wrote more about this process of "likening":

"I did liken all scriptures unto us, that it might be for our profit and learning. . . . Hear ye the words of the prophet, which were written unto all the house of Israel, and liken them unto yourselves" (1 Ne. 19:23–24). To "liken" a passage of scripture to oneself is to apply it to one's own circumstances. As both Nephi and Jacob explained, because Isaiah wrote about the house of Israel, others of Israel can use his words with specific application to their own situations. But to "liken" a scripture is not to assume that every statement of an ancient prophet must have a specific meaning in the latter-day setting. Nephi and Jacob set the correct pattern for interpreting Isaiah: They made wise application of the *principles* contained in Isaiah's words to their own circumstances.

Isaiah son of Amoz prophesied in Judah and Jerusalem for about fifty years, beginning around 740 B.C. The period in which he lived was a troubled time for the Israelites. Approximately two centuries earlier, the once-great empire of David and Solomon had been divided into two kingdoms, Israel in the north (consisting of the northern ten tribes) and Judah in the south (consisting of the tribes of Judah and Benjamin). In the early years of Isaiah's life, both kingdoms were prosperous, and each enjoyed, for the most part, political independence from the larger powers that surrounded them. But both Israel and Judah fell short of the Lord's standards of faith and righteousness, leading ultimately to their destruction. Isaiah lived to witness the judgments of God against the two kingdoms. Shortly after his ministry began, the Assyrian empire extended its influence into Palestine. Coming from the area of northern Mesopotamia (northern Iraq of today), the Assyrian kings created a large empire through extortion, conquest, and plunder. During Isaiah's ministry, both Israel and Judah became subjected to Assyria. Israel was soon destroyed as a nation, with the fall of its capital city Samaria in 721 B.C. Its cities were torn down, many people were killed, and many were taken away captive and relocated in other areas of the Assyrian empire (see 2 Kgs. 17). Throughout this period, Judah barely managed to survive. Isaiah constantly reminded its rulers and people to trust in the Lord and to reject alliances with other nations; the Assyrian threat would pass. It did pass, but as Isaiah prophesied, rebellion against Jehovah would not go without consequences. God would raise up another great threat, Babylon, which would execute divine judgment against God's rebellious people.[3]

THREE THEMES

Three principal themes are emphasized in Isaiah, and almost everything in the book fits into one of them:

Trust in the saving power of the Lord. Isaiah taught that God's saving power can be trusted in both temporal and spiritual things. We should trust in God to deliver us, not in man (e.g., Isa. 2:22; 12:2; 14:32). This message was especially important during the times that Judah was being threatened by foreign powers. When an alliance of Israel and Syria plotted to overthrow Judah, Isaiah's message was clear: Trust in God to deliver you, and the two nations you fear will be powerless against you. But do not trust in any other nation to come to your assistance (see Isa. 7:1–16; 8:1–4, 9–15; see also chapters 18; 20; 30–31). Even the great superpower, Assyria, is no match for the Lord, so trust in him rather than in alliances, politics, or armaments (see Isa. 10:24–34; chapters 36–37). Trusting in God's power to save us from earthly threats teaches us to trust in his power to save us from even greater dangers. Isaiah's words teach spiritual salvation at the same time they tell of temporal salvation, and some of the prophecies concerning the Messiah teach both important messages. The sign of God's deliverance of his people from temporal enemies— in chapter 7 the birth of a son—is also the sign of his deliverance of his people from sin and death (see Isa. 7:1–16). Messianic prophecies teach of the coming of a Deliverer. The salvation he brings requires us to exercise trust in him—"faith in the Lord Jesus Christ" (Article of Faith 4)—just as trusting him for earthly deliverance meant temporal salvation for ancient Israelites.

Covenant people have social and moral obligations. Isaiah spoke very often about the responsibility of society to care for the needs of its less fortunate members, particularly the widows and orphans. In ancient Near Eastern societies, including in Israel and Judah, women without husbands and children without fathers did not have the same economic security or protections that were enjoyed by others. Since the family connections of traditional households were not available to them, the law of Moses gave society as a whole the responsibility to care for them (e.g., Ex. 22:22–24; Deut. 14:28–29; 24:19–21). The abrogation of that responsibility was one of the Lord's chief complaints against his people in the book of Isaiah. Further, he condemned the rich who oppressed the poor, and he stressed integrity and other virtues (e.g., Isa. 3:13–15; 5:23; 10:1–4).

God's justice will prevail. Isaiah wrote more about this than about any other topic. He emphasized that the just would be vindicated and the unjust would be punished. In the immediate future of Isaiah's own people, God's justice would be shown in the destruction of the kingdom of Israel and in the calamities that would befall the kingdom of Judah. But with special emphasis on the Lord's coming in glory, Isaiah taught that the Lord's ultimate and worldwide justice will reward each with what he or she deserves: the wicked will be destroyed at the Lord's coming, and the righteous will live in millennial peace.[4] Through the New Testament and the scriptures of the Restoration, we know that God's justice calls for a Redeemer, one who would bear the consequences of the sins of all humanity so that imperfect mortals might be made worthy of God's blessings. Isaiah taught this redemption by means of magnificent "types" and "shadows"—

carefully veiled images that communicate truth to the spiritually mature who read with faith (e.g., chapter 53).

UNDERSTANDING ISAIAH

Some readers find the writings of Isaiah difficult to understand. More than one individual has read in the Book of Mormon as far as 2 Nephi 11 but has found it discouraging to proceed beyond that point, where thirteen straight chapters of Isaiah are quoted. It is not that Isaiah's doctrine is difficult. His doctrine is simple and straightforward—certainly easier than the very complex doctrinal treatments of Jacob and Nephi that precede and follow the Isaiah sections. The presumed difficulty with Isaiah lies in other areas. I believe that three factors cause some readers to find Isaiah challenging:

Lack of familiarity with the setting of Isaiah's day. This includes cultural, geographical, historical, and political conditions. Even though there is a timeless quality to Isaiah's words (more so, perhaps, than in the writings of any other Old Testament prophet), still his writings were recorded in a setting in world history that is very different from our own. Isaiah alludes constantly to the realities of his own day. Large sections of his record can be understood only in part without a knowledge of the history of his time and the political and social challenges that his people faced.[5] In the Book of Mormon, Nephi pointed out the importance of understanding Isaiah's world. He mentioned that he could understand Isaiah because of his knowledge of "the regions round about" and "the things of the Jews." "Yea, and my soul delighteth in the words of Isaiah, for I came out from Jerusalem, and mine eyes hath beheld the things of the Jews, and I know that the Jews do understand the things of the prophets, and there is none other people that understand the things which were spoken unto the Jews like unto them, save it be that they are taught after the manner of the things of the Jews. But behold, I, Nephi, have not taught my children after the manner of the Jews; but behold, I, of myself, have dwelt at Jerusalem, wherefore I know concerning the regions round about" (2 Ne. 25:5–6).

According to Nephi, no one can understand Isaiah's words as well as the Jews unless they are taught "the things of the Jews." He had an advantage because he knew those things, he had lived in Jerusalem, and he knew "the regions round about." Modern readers cannot know the world of ancient Jerusalem as well as he did, but there are things we can do to learn enough to understand Isaiah sufficiently. I recommend that readers turn first to the Bible itself to gain an understanding of Isaiah's day within the context of the Old Testament. Ideally, the place to start reading is at Genesis 1:1, from which one should read through the end of 2 Chronicles before beginning Isaiah. This 634-page warm-up would provide readers with indispensable background knowledge for understanding Isaiah. The recommendation may sound extreme, but from my experience, those who have paid this price do not find Isaiah to be mysterious, unlike those who pick out a random chapter and attempt to read it. For the historical and political context (and the book of Isaiah is full of history and politics), one should read at least from 1 Kings through 2 Chronicles before reading Isaiah—a mere 172-page warm-up.

Since modern readers generally do not know "the things of the Jews" and "the regions round about," I recommend careful attention to the Church's Bible maps and to a Bible dictionary that will provide summaries of useful information. Here is one reason why: In only the first seven Isaiah chapters quoted in the Book of Mormon (2 Ne. 12–18 = Isa. 2–8), readers are confronted with a host of names of persons, places, and things that will be unfamiliar to them—*Judah, Jerusalem, Philistines, Lebanon, Tarshish, Zion, bath, homer, ephah, Uzziah, seraphim, Ahaz, Jotham, Rezin, Syria, Pekah, Remaliah, Israel, Ephraim, Shearjashub, son of Tabael,*

Damascus, Immanuel, Assyria, Maher-shalal-hash-baz, Uriah, the prophetess, Samaria, and *Shiloah.* Some of these are incidental, but many are vital for understanding the chapters, just as knowing some of the following is for understanding the first seven sections of the Doctrine and Covenants—*Hiram, Ohio, my church, last days, Babylon, Joseph Smith, gospel, Nephites, Book of Mormon, my Spirit, saints, Manchester, New York, Moroni, Elijah, Harmony, Pennsylvania, Martin Harris, Zoramites, Lamanites, these records, Jesus Christ, Joseph Smith Sr., plates, Oliver Cowdery, Son of God, keys, disciples, Urim and Thummim, John the beloved, Peter, my kingdom,* and *James.* Imagine reading the Doctrine and Covenants with no idea of the meaning of those terms. The Bible dictionary in the LDS Bible is sufficient for most unfamiliar names and terms. A good one-volume Bible dictionary would provide more information, but multivolume Bible dictionaries generally provide too much, except for the most serious Bible readers.

Reading from Genesis on gives students of the Bible a *doctrinal* perspective that is not complete in the books of Kings and Chronicles and that is not available in most Bible dictionaries.[6] An understanding of key doctrinal matters such as the Abrahamic Covenant, the law of Moses, and the scattering and gathering of Israel is imperative for understanding Isaiah. But for each of those topics and for all other doctrinal topics, modern revelation provides a view that far exceeds that of the Bible. Before reading Isaiah, Latter-day Saints should know the Book of Mormon and the revelations of Joseph Smith to understand those doctrines.[7] The Book of Mormon is particularly significant, because in it important passages from Isaiah are quoted, after which Book of Mormon prophets present inspired commentary.

Lack of understanding of Isaiah's literary style. Modern readers are often surprised to learn that the revelations of the Old Testament prophets were written mostly in poetry. Isaiah is no exception. In the ancient Near East, including in Israel and Judah, when the various deities were perceived as speaking they usually did so in poetic style. To the ancient hearers and readers, poetry seemed to be the most appropriate means of expressing divine words. It conveyed, in their minds, a dignity, beauty, and reverence that could not be expressed in normal prose style, much as we now use, for the same reasons, an old form of English as the language of prayer. The most common feature of Hebrew poetry is what is called *parallelism*. In a typical poetic verse from the Bible, a concept is expressed twice, in two parallel phrases. The phrases most often mean approximately the same thing, but different words are used in each. The following example from Isaiah, arranged according to Isaiah's poetry, is illustrative (quotation marks added):

> And many people shall go and say, "Come ye, and
>   let us go up
> to the mountain of the Lord,
> to the house of the God of Jacob;
> and he will teach us of his ways,
> and we will walk in his paths":
> for out of Zion shall go forth the law,
> and the word of the Lord from Jerusalem.
> And he shall judge among the nations,
> and shall rebuke many people:
> and they shall beat their swords into plowshares,
> and their spears into pruning-hooks:
> nation shall not lift up sword against nation,
> neither shall they learn war any more. (Isa. 2:3–4)

Each of these couplets consists of two phrases. Though they are not always strictly synonymous in meaning, for the most part they are parallel in grammatical structure and message. This kind of parallelism is the basic building block of the poetic style of the Old Testament prophets. In some parallel couplets, the second phrase amplifies the first, or it teaches the same thing as the first but from a different angle. Usually the phrases complement each other in some manner.[8] Pondering the couplets together allows us to see the richness of Isaiah's message, especially as we allow the Spirit to teach us.

Isaiah's prophecies make very frequent use of *metaphor,* a category of literary style in which a word or phrase meaning one thing is used to represent something else, suggesting a likeness between them. An example is: "My well-beloved hath a vineyard in a very fruitful hill" (Isa. 5:1), the vineyard and its vines being identified in Isaiah 5:7 as Israel and Judah. Similarly, the king of Assyria, with his ever-expanding empire, is described graphically in Isaiah 8:7–8 as a river flooding over its banks: "the waters of the river, strong and many . . . ; and he shall come up over all his channels, and go over all his banks. And he shall pass through Judah; he shall overflow and go over." A great latter-day leader, undoubtedly Joseph Smith, is called a "root" (a shoot that grows off the main stem) and an "ensign" (a banner, or rallying point), to whom the nations will gather.

A *simile* is an application of metaphor that uses words such as *like,* or *as:* Israel will be "*as* the sand of the sea" (Isa. 10:22), while Babylon will be "*as* when God overthrew Sodom and Gomorrah" (Isa. 13:19). An *allegory* is a metaphor in story form. Isaiah's story of the vineyard in Isaiah 5 is an allegory, and most of Jesus' parables in the New Testament are allegories.

Modern readers sometimes mistake biblical metaphor for "symbolism" and see it as a code for concealing mysteries. Instead, it is simply good writing that communicates well within its own cultural framework. Sometimes it is intended to be elegant, artistic, and evocative, and sometimes it is intended to be graphic and forceful. But it is intended to be understood. While our own culture uses it less freely than did the people of the Bible, metaphor is still part of our world today. Understandable examples would include the following: "The apostles are *pillars* in the Church," or "The prophet is *a watchman on the tower.*" The metaphors suggest a *likeness* between the persons and some characteristic of the object, but they do not suggest an equation. Frequently a metaphor is intended only to bring forth a general feeling, or a fleeting visual image. Rarely are details important or intended to be analyzed. We know that the apostles are not made of granite or of reinforced concrete, nor does the prophet have a tower from which he watches. Modern readers sometimes abuse Isaiah's words by attempting to see in them details that the prophet himself undoubtedly never had in mind.

Many scriptures can be rightly understood in more than one way. Nephi said that Isaiah's words pertain to "things both temporal and spiritual" (1 Ne. 22:3). Wise readers, guided by the Spirit, need to be sensitive to multiple applications and fulfillments.[9]

Difficulty with translation. Another reason why English-speaking Latter-day Saints find Isaiah difficult is the old language of the King James translation, which was first published in 1611 but which reflects the language of even earlier translations.[10] Most of the spelling of our current King James Version dates from revisions of the late 1700s and differs substantially from the 1611 original. The punctuation is different in thousands of places, but the words remain virtually identical to those of the first King James Version. Thus its language is still very archaic, making understanding a challenge for most readers. English has changed so much since the early seventeenth century that modern readers often have difficulty with both the grammar and the vocabulary of the King James text. This is especially true in the prophetic books, like Isaiah, because of the richness of vocabulary and the difficulty of grammar in poetic writing. In some ways, the great strengths and beauties of the King James Version are more apparent in the Gospels and in other prose narratives of the Bible. Some readers

have found that reading Isaiah in a good modern translation elimi-
nates much of the difficulty of understanding it.[11]

Nephi added some additional information about reading the
words of Isaiah. While the Jews in Jerusalem could understand
Isaiah's writings (see 2 Ne. 25:5), Nephi's own people found
them very difficult. He explained why: "For they know not concerning the manner of prophesying among the Jews" (2 Ne. 25:1).
Nephi had endeavored *not* to teach his people the ways of those
from whom he had come, "for their works were works of darkness" (2 Ne. 25:2; see also v. 6). The New World culture of Nephi
and his people was to begin with a clean slate, except for the
much-needed sacred influences of the plates of brass. One thing
that seems to have been lost in the process was "the manner of
prophesying among the Jews." Though he never explained what
he meant by that phrase, Nephi presented his own style as a contrast. While Isaiah's prophecies were "not plain," Nephi prophesied "according to the plainness which hath been with me from
the time that I came out from Jerusalem with my father; for
behold, my soul delighteth in plainness unto my people, that they
may learn" (2 Ne. 25:4). He wrote "according to my plainness; in
the which I know that no man can err" (2 Ne. 25:7). Whereas
Isaiah's words were written in a sophisticated literary form with
abundant use of carefully crafted poetic styles and images, Nephi's
words are "plain" and to the point. The "manner of prophesying
among the Jews," then, probably has reference to the literary style
in which the Israelite and Judahite prophets preserved the Lord's
word. The Book of Mormon does not continue the writing style of
the Hebrew prophets. While it is a literary masterpiece in its own
right, its presentation of the words of God and of the prophets is
very different from that of the Old Testament. The revelations
of the Book of Mormon, though unparalleled in their depth,
power, and message, are presented in a clear, careful, and "plain"

manner, that those who read them "may learn" more effectively (see 2 Ne. 25:4).

Nephi's final qualification for understanding Isaiah is not exceeded in its importance by any other. Isaiah's words, he wrote, "are plain unto all those that are filled with the spirit of prophecy" (2 Ne. 25:4). That spirit of prophecy is the spirit of revelation that is available to anyone who has the Holy Ghost and the testimony of Jesus (see Rev. 19:10). It is an indispensable element for understanding Isaiah. Those who read Isaiah with the Holy Ghost will see in its pages a testimony of the Lord, of his love, and of his work to bless his children. They will then be taught truths that they could not learn otherwise.

NOTES

1. Altogether, almost one-third of the book of Isaiah is quoted or paraphrased in the Book of Mormon. See Monte S. Nyman, *"Great Are the Words of Isaiah"* (Salt Lake City: Bookcraft, 1980), 283.

2. The fullest LDS treatments of the book of Isaiah are Victor L. Ludlow, *Isaiah: Prophet, Seer, and Poet* (Salt Lake City: Deseret Book, 1982), and Donald W. Parry, Jay A. Parry, and Tina M. Peterson, *Understanding Isaiah* (Salt Lake City: Deseret Book, 1998). Helpful in showing how Isaiah has been interpreted by leaders of the Church is Nyman, *"Great Are the Words of Isaiah."* LDS discussions of Isaiah are found in Kent P. Jackson, ed., *First Kings to Malachi*, vol. 4 in Studies in Scripture series (Salt Lake City: Deseret Book, 1993), 80–164.

3. For background, see Jackson, *First Kings to Malachi*, 20–45, 75–79, 165–77.

4. See Isaiah 2:4, 10–21; 3:1–8, 10–26; 4:1–6; 5:5–6, 25–30; 7:17–25; 8:6–8; 9:1–21; 10:5–19, 24–27; 11:6–9, 14–16; 13:1–22; 14:1–32.

5. For example, Isaiah 7:1–8:10; 10:5–19, 24–34; 13:1–5, 14–22; 14:3–31.

6. The Bible dictionary of the LDS edition of the Bible is, of course, an exception. Its brief doctrinal entries are excellent.

7. I have attempted to summarize the teachings of modern revelation on these and other topics in the present volume and in my *The Restored Gospel and the Book of Genesis* (Salt Lake City: Deseret Book, 2001).

8. For a convenient discussion of different types of parallelism, see Ludlow, *Isaiah: Prophet, Seer, and Poet,* 31–39. An important work on Hebrew parallelism is Robert Alter, *The Art of Biblical Poetry* (New York: Basic Books, 1985).

9. See Dallin H. Oaks, "Scripture Reading and Revelation," *Ensign,* January 1995, 8.

10. See David Daniell, *The Bible in English* (New Haven: Yale University Press, 2003), 427–60; F. F. Bruce, *History of the Bible in English From the Earliest Versions* (New York: Oxford University Press, 1978), 12–112; S. L. Greenslade, "English Versions of the Bible, 1525–1611," in *The Cambridge History of the Bible: The West from the Reformation to the Present Day,* ed. S. L. Greenslade (Cambridge: Cambridge University Press, 1963), 164–68.

11. When the New English Bible (NEB) was produced, its translators sacrificed doctrinal and linguistic accuracy in their attempt to achieve literary quality. In my view, they failed at that too, as they did also with their more recent Revised English Bible (REB). The Revised Standard Version (RSV) and its updated New Revised Standard Version (NRSV) are excellent, linguistically reliable translations, but to me they do not seem to be as successful as the King James Version or the New International Version at conveying the feeling of reverence and devotion that belongs in a translation of the Bible. The New King James Version (New KJV) is a recommendable update of the King James translation that modernizes some of the old vocabulary and grammar of the KJV. In my view the best modern English translation of the Bible is the New International Version (NIV). This translation was made by a committee of scholars whose belief in the inspiration of the Bible is apparent throughout their work. It is translated in a beautiful literary style that is at the same time very reliable and accurate linguistically. And it expresses an impressive sense of faith, dignity, devotion, and reverence for the things of God.

9

THE ROD AND ROOT OF JESSE

D octrine and Covenants 113 sheds light on some prophecies of Isaiah in a unique way. In it, questions are asked concerning some of Isaiah's words, and the Lord's answers are given.[1] Isaiah 11 is a prophecy with a latter-day orientation that deals with both the period of the Restoration, in which we now live, and the Millennium. The ancient revelation speaks of the millennial world in which the wolf, the lamb, the leopard, and the kid will lie down in peace together (see Isa. 11:6) and in which the earth will be full of the knowledge of the Lord (see Isa. 11:9). Prior to that day, the day of restoration would come—the period of time in which the Lord would begin the work which would culminate in millennial glory.

Three questions regarding this revelation are asked and answered in Doctrine and Covenants 113:1–6:

Question: "Who is the Stem of Jesse?" (v. 1).

Answer: "It is Christ" (v. 2).

Question: "What is the rod . . . that should come of the Stem of Jesse?" (v. 3).

Answer: "It is a servant in the hands of Christ, who is partly a descendant of Jesse as well as of Ephraim, or of the house of Joseph, on whom there is laid much power" (v. 4).

Question: "What is the root of Jesse?" (v. 5).

Answer: "It is a descendant of Jesse, as well as of Joseph, unto whom rightly belongs the priesthood, and the keys of the kingdom, for an ensign, and for the gathering of my people in the last days" (v. 6).

These words have been given a variety of interpretations by Latter-day Saint authors. The answer to the first question is quite explicit: the "Stem of Jesse" is Jesus Christ. But the second and third questions are discussed most often.[2] The evidence seems clear that both the "rod out of the stem of Jesse" (Isa. 11:1) and the "root of Jesse" (Isa. 11:10) refer to the same individual—the Prophet Joseph Smith. In Isaiah's prophecy, *stem* is translated from the Hebrew word *geza'*. It means "trunk" and represents the main body of the tree. The word *rod* comes from the Hebrew *ḥōṭer* and means "branch," or "twig." It grows from the trunk. The *root*, Hebrew *šōreš*, simply means "root." Even though the tree starts with a root, eventually the roots, like the branches, grow out from the trunk of the tree. Thus the trunk of the tree is Christ, and both the branch and the root are his extensions. A comparison of the descriptions given in Doctrine and Covenants 113:4 and 6 leads to the conclusion that they both refer to the same person.

Rod Out of the Stem of Jesse	Root of Jessee
"A servant in the hands of Christ"	
"Partly a descendant of Jesse as well as of Ephraim, or of the house of Joseph"	"A descendant of Jessee, as well as of Joseph"
"On whom there is laid much power"	"Unto whom rightly belongs the priesthood, and the keys of the kingdom"
	"For an ensign, and for the gathering of my people in the last days"

The two descriptions complement each other, with the description of the root generally amplifying that of the rod. That the root is a servant in the hands of the Lord, as is mentioned concerning the rod, is clear from the characteristics of his calling that are given in verse 6. Both the rod and the root are descendants of both Jesse and Joseph. Both have important power. The power of the root is specified as being the keys of the kingdom and a right to the priesthood, and the work of the root is associated with the latter-day gathering. Perhaps it is not necessary to determine how the rod and root metaphors fit together, because they are actually found in separate parts of the prophecy, if not in separate prophecies. If Isaiah 11:10 begins a new prophecy of the gathering, it continues the tree metaphor of the first part of the chapter. The root is not necessarily the ancestor of the rod. While the flow of nutrients from the soil follows the order *root* → *trunk* → *twig,* at the same time the life-giving chemicals produced through photosynthesis flow in the order *twig* → *trunk* → *root.* Thus there is no need to assume a genealogical sequence from root to twig. In fact, both the twig and the root branch off equally from the trunk. In the Old Testament and in other Near Eastern texts, *root* is used sometimes to mean "offspring," rather than "ancestor," because it stems from the body of the plant, as does the twig.[3] Thus "root of Jesse" does not necessarily mean Jesse's ancestor, which Joseph Smith clearly was not.

The rod is identified as "partly a descendant of Jesse as well as of Ephraim, or of the house of Joseph" (D&C 113:4). The root is called "a descendant of Jesse, as well as of Joseph" (D&C 113:6). We have no scriptural knowledge of Joseph Smith's heritage from Jesse other than that given in the verses under consideration here. Jesse, the father of David, was the ancestor of all the kings of Judah, including Jesus Christ. But perhaps the descent from this royal line connotes something other than, or in addition to, genealogical ancestry. Jesus was Israel's king. He conferred the keys of the kingdom on his ancient apostles (see Matt. 16:19), and Peter, James, and John conferred those same keys on Joseph Smith. Thus, as a priesthood bearer traces the descent of his priesthood authority through those before him, Joseph Smith's line of authority pertaining to the keys of the kingdom traces back to the royal line of ancient Jesse. At the council of priesthood leaders and key holders that will yet be held at Adam-ondi-Ahman, Joseph Smith and his successors will return the keys of the kingdom to father Adam, who, representing the entire human family, will return the kingdom to its rightful king, the Lord Jesus Christ (see chapter 18 in this volume).

The priesthood and the keys of the kingdom "rightly belong" to the root—the latter-day descendant of Jesse and Joseph. Through revelation we know of Joseph Smith's descent from ancient Joseph (see 2 Ne. 3:7; JST Gen. 50:27–28), and the Lord affirmed to his prophet that he and his co-workers were heirs of the priesthood and had inherited their right to it through lineal descent. "Thus saith the Lord unto you, with whom the priesthood hath continued through the lineage of your fathers—For ye are lawful heirs, according to the flesh. . . . Therefore your life and the priesthood have remained, and must needs remain through you and your lineage" (D&C 86:8–10). This principle is born out also in Doctrine and Covenants 113:8, in which the Lord tells us that the latter-day Zion "has a right" to "the authority of the priesthood" "by lineage." When Moroni appeared to young Joseph Smith during the night of 21–22 September 1823, he quoted Isaiah 11, saying "that it was about to be fulfilled" (JS–H 1:40). The fulfillment was underway at that very moment, as the Prophet was receiving instruction and training that would lead to the restoration of all things.

Jesus said, "I am the vine, ye are the branches" (John 15:5). Joseph Smith, as a "rod" or "branch"—"a servant in the hands of Christ" whose work stands as "an ensign, and for the gathering of

[God's] people in the last days" (D&C 113:4, 6)—fulfills the beginning of Isaiah's great prophecy. But the ultimate fulfillment will be in a millennial setting, when Christ himself reigns as king on earth, in "the spirit of wisdom and understanding, the spirit of counsel and might, [and] the spirit of knowledge" (Isa. 11:2). It will be then that "the wolf also shall dwell with the lamb, and the leopard shall lie down with the kid; and the calf and the young lion and the fatling together; and a little child shall lead them." Then "the earth shall be full of the knowledge of the Lord, as the waters cover the sea" (Isa. 11:6, 9).

Notes

1. For background of the revelation, see Joseph Smith, *History of The Church of Jesus Christ of Latter-day Saints*, ed. B. H. Roberts, 2d ed. rev., 7 vols. (Salt Lake City: The Church of Jesus Christ of Latter-day Saints, 1932–51), 3:8–10; and Lyndon W. Cook, *The Revelations of the Prophet Joseph Smith* (Provo, Utah: Seventy's Mission Bookstore, 1981), 224–25.

2. See Victor L. Ludlow, *Isaiah: Prophet, Seer, and Poet* (Salt Lake City: Deseret Book, 1981), 167–78; Monte S. Nyman, *"Great Are the Words of Isaiah"* (Salt Lake City: Bookcraft, 1980), 71–74; Sidney B. Sperry, *The Voice of Israel's Prophets* (Salt Lake City: Deseret Book, 1952), 33–37.

3. See, for example, the inscription of Azitiwada of the Danunians of Karatepe, who refers (apparently) to the king's son as the "root" of his father; see J. C. L. Gibson, *Textbook of Syrian Semitic Inscriptions, vol. 3, Phoenician Inscriptions* (Oxford: Clarendon, 1982), 46–47, 57–58 (Azitiwada Inscription, line 10).

10

Joseph Smith and the Lord's Servant in Isaiah

The restored gospel illuminates the writings of biblical prophets because in the pages of modern revelation we have a clearer view of doctrinal truth. In the Restoration's light, we can see better the ancient prophetic messages, including the prophecies of future events. The Doctrine and Covenants contains many revelations that touch on biblical themes, and some of the sections reflect specifically on the words of Isaiah, the prophet of Jerusalem in the eighth century before Christ.[1] Similarly, the Book of Mormon draws from, alludes to, and explains some of Isaiah's revelations. Isaiah 49:1–6, for example, is a revelation that contains great prophecies of our time. Latter-day revelations—in the Book of Mormon and the Doctrine and Covenants—open its meaning to our understanding.

A Latter-day Servant

Isaiah 49 is a "servant" prophecy, one of several in the latter part of Isaiah in which there is a focus on the work of a servant whom the Lord has chosen to do his will. Usually the servant's identity is not specified in the revelation, so sometimes more than one interpretation is valid. When God made covenants with Abraham, Isaac, and Jacob, he called them to bless the world through their service.

They and their descendants became "chosen people," that is, people called with a special calling (see Abr. 2:9–11). Members of the house of Israel are called to represent the Lord in service to others. On the most basic level, Israel itself seems to fit the description of the Lord's chosen servant in Isaiah: "Thou, Israel, art my servant, Jacob whom I have chosen, the seed of Abraham my friend" (Isa. 41:8); "Yet now hear, O Jacob my servant; and Israel, whom I have chosen" (Isa. 44:1).[2] Jesus taught his disciples how they should serve: "Ye are the salt of the earth" (Matt. 5:13); "Ye are the light of the world" (Matt. 5:14); "Feed my sheep" (John 21:16).

Just as the Lord has called Israel collectively to be his servant, some individuals within Israel have been called to a more specific level of service. Some of Isaiah's servant passages may find more appropriate application to the mission of the prophets, rather than to Israel at large. The prophets are servants within God's servant nation. Finally, Jesus Christ himself is *the* Servant; it is in him that Isaiah's servant passages find their most complete fulfillment. Jesus is the source of all the good gifts with which his servants minister. He is the light of the world in the fullest way. The light that the prophets and the house of Israel possess simply reflects his character and glory—the source of all true light. Similarly, though his servants have been called to feed his sheep (see John 21:16), he himself is the Good Shepherd (see John 10:14). Since all good things and all good people are types of Christ and reflect his nature, perhaps we can identify the servant of whom Isaiah wrote on different levels, depending on the information provided: the house of Israel collectively, the prophets, and the Lord himself. Some of the passages seem to apply to more than one of these.[3] The revelation in Isaiah 49 deals, among other things, with the role of Israel in a latter-day setting and perhaps specifically with Israel's leader and representative—the Prophet Joseph Smith.

The King James Version text reads as follows (quotation marks added):[4]

Listen, O isles, unto me;
and hearken, ye people, from far;
The Lord hath called me from the womb;
from the bowels of my mother hath he made men-
     tion of my name.
And he hath made my mouth like a sharp sword;
in the shadow of his hand hath he hid me,
and made me a polished shaft;
in his quiver hath he hid me;
And said unto me, "Thou art my servant,
O Israel, in whom I will be glorified."
Then I said, "I have laboured in vain,
I have spent my strength for nought, and in vain:
yet surely my judgment is with the Lord,
and my work with my God." (Isa. 49:1–4)

"Called me from the womb" (Isa. 49:1). From the days of the
Patriarchs, ancient Joseph and his descendants had been singled
out to stand at the head of the house of Israel (see Gen. 37:5–11;
48:13–20; 49:26; Deut. 33:16–17). An important part of that calling included the responsibility to be saviors of their brethren of
Israel, just as their forefather Joseph had been a temporal savior
in ancient times (see JST Gen. 48:8–11).

"In the shadow of his hand hath he hid me" (Isa. 49:2). At the same
time that Jacob pronounced the blessing of presidency on Joseph and
his posterity, he prophesied that government and rule would be in
the hands of the tribe of Judah (see Gen. 49:8–10). That was fulfilled
in the kingship of David and his descendants and will be fulfilled to
its fullest measure in the millennial kingship of Jesus Christ. In biblical times, the descendants of Joseph never ruled over all the house
of Israel, despite their inherited keys of presidency. As far as we know,
Ephraim's presidency over Israel was never to be realized until the
latter days. With the calling of Joseph Smith, a descendant of
Ephraim, the tribe to which he belonged took its position of service
in the family of Israel. Foreordained to this latter-day labor, Joseph's

children—both of Ephraim and of Manasseh—have accepted their calling to bring the blessings of the gospel to their brethren.

"A polished shaft . . . in his quiver" (Isa. 49:2). Joseph Smith is reported to have provided an interpretation that may show his own identification with Isaiah's words: "I am like a huge, rough stone rolling down from a high mountain; and the only polishing I get is when some corner gets rubbed off by coming in contact with something else . . . all hell knocking off a corner here and a corner there. Thus I will become a smooth and polished shaft in the quiver of the Almighty."[5]

"Thou art my servant" (Isa. 49:3). The speaker, called Israel, explains his calling and what God has done for him to enable him to fulfill it. The Lord calls him "my servant . . . in whom I will be glorified," in a setting that is clearly in the future. Israel pointed out that his labors in the past had been in vain (see Isa. 49:4), to which the Lord responded with a powerful prophecy of more significant service that lay ahead.

> And now, saith the Lord
> that formed me from the womb to be his
> servant,
> to bring Jacob again to him,
> Though Israel be not gathered,
> yet shall I be glorious in the eyes of the Lord,
> and my God shall be my strength.
> And he said, "It is a light thing that thou shouldest
> be my servant
> to raise up the tribes of Jacob,
> and to restore the preserved of Israel:
> I will also give thee for a light to the Gentiles,
> that thou mayest be my salvation unto the end of
> the earth." (Isa. 49:5–6)

Israel's assigned task, as specified in these verses, is in two parts, each one constituting a major mission to a group of God's children: (1) to reestablish Israel and gather it again to the Lord, and (2) to serve as "a light to the Gentiles," thereby making salvation available to them also. The word *Gentiles* in the Old Testament means "peoples" or "nations." It includes all the people of the world who are not of Israel. The mission of the Lord's servant is thus to bring salvation not only to Israel but also to everyone else.

"*To bring Jacob again to him*" (Isa. 49:5), "*to raise up the tribes of Jacob, and to restore the preserved of Israel*" (Isa. 49:6). The restoration of the house of Israel is one of the great events of the last days, and the servant could rejoice in his privilege to participate. In modern times, the keys of the gathering were restored to the presiding officer of the tribe of Ephraim, the Prophet Joseph Smith (see D&C 110:11). It is under the authority of those keys that the gathering takes place today and will continue. Jeremiah looked upon the latter-day restoration as being far greater than the Lord's gathering of his people the first time from Egypt. So great would be this new latter-day exodus that the old one in the days of Moses would soon be forgotten (see Jer. 16:14–15). Jeremiah also foretold that it would be "the watchmen upon the mount Ephraim" who would cry, "Arise ye, and let us go up to Zion unto the Lord our God" (Jer. 31:6). In modern revelation, the Lord has affirmed that gathered Israelites will return and receive their blessings under the hand of "the children of Ephraim" (D&C 133:30; see also vv. 26–34). Today it is, with not many exceptions, Ephraim and Manasseh who constitute the Lord's Church and who are taking the gospel message to their brothers and sisters—other scattered remnants of the house of Israel.

"*To bring Jacob again to him, Though Israel be not gathered*" (Isa. 49:5). The King James Version is difficult in this verse, as is the Hebrew on which it is based. A seemingly better-preserved Hebrew original in the Qumran Isaiah Scroll (1QIs^a) may provide a more likely translation: "to bring Jacob back to him and gather Israel to himself."

"A light to the Gentiles" (Isa. 49:6). The Lord's servant learned that the gathering of Israel would be too easy a task, and something even more amazing would be required of him.[6] He would be called to take salvation to the rest of the world also. Nephi and others taught how the gospel blessings of the latter days would be made available not only to the house of Israel but to non-Israelites, the Gentiles, as well (see 1 Ne. 22:8–11). Modern revelation tells us that the Church in the latter days is to take the saving message to *all* people (see JS–M 1:31; D&C 42:58; 133:37). Today Joseph Smith, his successors, and the descendants of Ephraim and Manasseh stand out as the main participants in this work.

Whether we speak of Israel or of the nations of the world, the Restoration teaches us that the essence of the gathering is the gathering to the covenants of the gospel of Jesus Christ. As Nephi taught, to be gathered means to come to Christ (see 1 Ne. 10:14). Because such phrases as "the gathering of Israel" usually refer to joining the Lord's Church, scriptural images of a physical return to ancestral lands may often represent returning to ancestral covenants, accepting the gospel, and joining The Church of Jesus Christ of Latter-day Saints. Today the gathering of Israel is taking place as individuals from all over the earth are gathering among the Saints in their own lands. And Gentiles, those who are not of literal Israelite descent, are equally welcome.

Modern revelation in Doctrine and Covenants 86:8–11 clarifies Isaiah's prophecy and identifies Joseph Smith and his co-workers of the tribes of Joseph—members of the Church of Jesus Christ—as the fulfillment of the words of Isaiah. According to the revelation, the Lord's latter-day servants are they "with whom the priesthood hath continued through the lineage of [their] fathers—For [they] are lawful heirs, according to the flesh, and have been hid from the world with Christ in God" (D&C 86:8–9). Having been foreordained to this calling, and having inherited it through lineal descent, ancient Joseph's children now are no longer "hid from the world" (D&C 86:9) "in the shadow of [the Lord's] hand" but are at the forefront of his work in the last days. They are restoring scattered Israel to the covenant blessings, and they are bringing the message of the gospel to the Gentiles as well, to "every nation, and kindred, and tongue, and people" (D&C 133:37). The Lord concluded his revelation to Joseph Smith and the Church: "Therefore, blessed are ye if ye continue in my goodness, a light unto the Gentiles, and through this priesthood, a savior unto my people Israel" (D&C 86:11).

NOTES

1. A list of passages from Isaiah reflected in the Doctrine and Covenants is found in Monte S. Nyman, *"Great Are the Words of Isaiah"* (Salt Lake City: Bookcraft, 1980), 289–91.

2. Note how "Israel," "Jacob," and "the seed of Abraham" are synonymous in these passages.

3. A good and convenient summary of the "Servant" issue is found in W. S. LaSor, D. A. Hubbard, and F. W. Bush, *Old Testament Survey* (Grand Rapids, Mich.: Eerdmans, 1982), 392–95.

4. The text is formatted according to Isaiah's Hebrew poetry.

5. Joseph Smith, *History of The Church of Jesus Christ of Latter-day Saints*, ed. B. H. Roberts, 2d ed. rev., 7 vols. (Salt Lake City: The Church of Jesus Christ of Latter-day Saints, 1932–51), 5:401. The origin of the statement is unknown; see Andrew F. Ehat and Lyndon W. Cook, eds., *The Words of Joseph Smith: The Contemporary Accounts of the Nauvoo Discourses of the Prophet Joseph* (Provo, Utah: Religious Studies Center, Brigham Young University, 1980), 205, 282 n. 7.

6. The King James Version phrase "a light thing" (Isa. 49:6) means "a *small* thing" or "an *insignificant* thing." The word *light* in "a light to the Gentiles" is translated from a different Hebrew word and means "light."

11

NURSING FATHERS AND NURSING MOTHERS

Isaiah 49:14–23 is a prophecy of special distinction in light of modern revelation. Two Book of Mormon prophets provided commentary on it, explaining its meaning and allowing us to gain important insights into the Lord's work. This is a revelation about Zion. In the Old Testament, *Zion* usually is a name for Jerusalem. Typically it applies to Jerusalem in a latter-day setting, and often it is used in the context of Jerusalem's restored and sanctified state. As with other place names, sometimes it applies to the inhabitants and not just to the place. But because Zion is a type as well as a location, we can apply its characteristics in other contexts, as we liken scriptures to ourselves (see 1 Ne. 19:24). In this revelation, Zion is depicted as a mother bereaved of her children, "forsaken" and "forgotten." But just as a mother cannot forget her child, the Lord cannot forget Zion, his chosen one. Her memory is ever before him, and he will bless her according to her desires.[1]

> Behold, I have graven thee upon the palms of my
>   hands;
> thy walls are continually before me.
> Thy children shall make haste. . . .
> Lift up thine eyes round about,

and behold: all these gather themselves together,
and come to thee.
As I live, saith the Lord, thou shalt surely clothe
   thee with them all,
as with an ornament, and bind them on thee, as a
   bride doeth. (Isa. 49:16–18)

The return of Zion's lost children will be so dramatic that she will hardly be prepared to receive them. In her joy, excitement, and bewilderment she asks,

Who hath begotten me these,
seeing I have lost my children, and am desolate,
a captive, and removing to and fro?
and who hath brought up these?
Behold, I was left alone;
these, where had they been? (Isa. 49:21; cf.
   54:1–3)

The Lord answers in an important revelation that tells of the work of latter-day Gentiles in bringing about Israel's gathering and restoration:

Behold, I will lift up mine hand to the Gentiles,
and set up my standard to the people:
and they shall bring thy sons in their arms,
and thy daughters shall be carried upon their
   shoulders.
And kings shall be thy nursing fathers,
and their queens thy nursing mothers. (Isa.
   49:22–23)

The Book of Mormon provides the keys to understanding Isaiah's words. Nephi, who recognized that Isaiah's prophecies are fulfilled in "temporal and spiritual" ways (1 Ne. 22:3), foresaw the Gentiles contributing to the temporal blessing of his descendants and others of the house of Israel. But he also saw them blessing Israel in an even more important way—spiritually. According to Nephi, the fulfillment of Isaiah's prophecy of nursing fathers and mothers will be "the making known of the covenants of the Father," "in bringing about his covenants and his gospel unto those who are of the house of Israel" (1 Ne. 22:9, 11). The kings and queens and fathers and mothers who will nurture Israel will be those who bring them the gospel of Jesus Christ, a prophecy that is being fulfilled in our time. The fulfillment began with the Restoration and continues as missionaries from Gentile nations take the saving message to Lehi's descendants and others of the house of Israel, eventually including the Jews. Being "brought out of obscurity and out of darkness," the once-lost covenant people are thus learning that Jesus Christ "is their Savior and their Redeemer, the Mighty One of Israel" (1 Ne. 22:12).

To Nephi's brother Jacob, the Lord revealed a specific meaning of Isaiah's prophecy of the Gentiles blessing Israel that will yet be fulfilled. Speaking of the Jews, the Lord said: "When the day cometh that they shall believe in me, that I am Christ, then have I covenanted with their fathers that they shall be restored in the flesh, upon the earth unto the lands of their inheritance. And it shall come to pass that they shall be gathered in from their long dispersion, from the isles of the sea, and from the four parts of the earth; and the nations of the Gentiles shall be great in the eyes of me, saith God, in carrying them forth to the lands of their inheritance. Yea, the kings of the Gentiles shall be nursing fathers unto them, and their queens shall become nursing mothers" (2 Ne. 10:7–9).

Thus for the Jews, for the children of Lehi, and for all the house of Israel, the Book of Mormon shows that Isaiah's message has two fulfillments—one spiritual and one temporal. In the latter days, the Lord's servants among the Gentiles will take the message of the restored gospel to all branches of Israel. They will teach them the principles of salvation, establish Christ's Church among them, and administer to them the covenants and ordinances of the gospel. They will be to them the nursing fathers and mothers of which Isaiah prophesied, bringing the scattered remnants of Israel in their arms and on their shoulders to the Savior, to the covenants of the gospel, and to the blessings of the Church of Jesus Christ. When those remnants of Israel accept the gospel and its blessings, then will the Lord remember his other covenants made to their fathers, and they will be restored to their promised lands. All of this will happen by means of the priesthood keys of gathering, restored to the Church through the Prophet Joseph Smith (see D&C 110:11).

NOTE

1. In these passages, the King James Version text is formatted according to Isaiah's Hebrew poetry.

12

THE LATTER-DAY DAVID

The Old Testament contains powerful metaphors of sheep and shepherds (e.g. Jer. 23:1; 31:10; 50:6, 17; Ezek. 34:1–31). Shepherds are leaders, those in whose care God has entrusted his children. In ancient Israel and Judah, those leaders included the prophets, the priests, and the kings, individuals charged with the responsibility of providing leadership within their respective spheres. Unfortunately, the Bible shows evidence for all-too-frequent corruption in each of these areas (e.g., Ezek. 22:26–28; Zeph. 3:3–4; Micah 3:11). Because the shepherds were not worthy of their callings, the Lord told Ezekiel that God himself would become Israel's shepherd and gather his flock:

> Behold, I, even I, will both search my sheep, and
> seek them out.
> As a shepherd seeketh out his flock in the day that
> he is among his sheep that are scattered;
> so will I seek out my sheep,
> and will deliver them out of all places where they
> have been scattered in the cloudy and dark day.
> And I will bring them out from the people,
> and gather them from the countries,
> and will bring them to their own land,

and feed them upon the mountains of Israel by the
   rivers,
and in all the inhabited places of the country.
I will feed them in a good pasture,
and upon the high mountains of Israel shall their
   fold be. (Ezek. 34:11–14)[1]

The message of the gathering of Israel is clear in this passage.
The lost sheep of Israel will be brought back to the fold—gathered
"out from the people" and "from the countries." They will be
restored to the covenants of the gospel with Jehovah himself, their
true prophet, priest, and king, as their shepherd.

When Jesus proclaimed himself to be the "good shepherd"
(John 10:11, 14), he was drawing upon the divine shepherd
imagery familiar to the Jews from the Old Testament. Thus he was
saying much more than simply "Follow me." Israel's Good
Shepherd was Jehovah himself, as the Jews knew, and Jesus' pro-
nouncement was a statement of that fact. In saying it, he was pro-
claiming that he is God: 'I Am Jehovah.' As he punctuated the
announcement with the phrase, "I and my Father are one," the
Jews "took up stones again to stone him" (John 10:30–31). In
modern revelation the message is the same. The Lord told Joseph
Smith and the early Latter-day Saints: "I am the good shepherd"
(D&C 50:44).

THE MILLENNIAL KING

Ezekiel received a powerful revelation about the Lord's millennial rule among his people:

I will set up one shepherd over them,
and he shall feed them, even my servant David;
he shall feed them, and he shall be their shepherd.
And I the Lord will be their God,

and my servant David a prince among them. (Ezek.
  34:23–24)

In another revelation the Lord said, "David my servant shall
be king over them; and they all shall have one shepherd. . . . And
my servant David shall be their prince for ever" (Ezek. 37:24, 25;
see also Jer. 30:9; 33:14–22; Hosea 3:5). Joseph Smith taught that
"the throne and kingdom of David" would be "given to another
by the name of David in the last days, raised up out of his lineage."[2] Recently it has been suggested by some that the millennial
David, who will be Israel's "shepherd" (Ezek. 34:23), "king," and
"prince for ever" (Ezek. 37:25), will be someone other than Jesus
Christ. This idea is nowhere to be found in the scriptures, and it
contradicts clear revealed evidence. It appears to come from a mis-
interpretation of poetic images in the Old Testament, where
metaphors such as *branch, shepherd,* and *David* are used inter-
changeably with words like *king* and *prince* with regard to Israel's
millennial ruler.[3] There is no mystery involved in the identity of
the millennial king David. The passages refer to Jesus Christ, who
was a descendant of David in the flesh and who is and ever will
be the true Shepherd and King of Israel.

In the minds of ancient Israelites, David—the shepherd who
became king—embodied the very essence of kingship for several
reasons. He was appointed by revelation from God, during his
reign Israel and Judah were united as one nation under one king,
he ruled as a powerful and popular monarch, he defeated all enemies and introduced a period of peace and prosperity, and the
Lord's sanctuary was among the people. These things came to
mind whenever David's name was mentioned, and they provided
for later Israelites not only the reminiscence of a past golden age
but also the longing for a future age that would be even more glorious.[4] Thus the name *David* became a metaphor for ideal kingship and was fittingly applied to Israel's millennial Monarch. The

millennial King would be, as it were, a second King David, restoring the glories of the past to which later generations of Israel looked with longing. "The Holy One of Israel," wrote Nephi, will "reign in dominion, and might, and power, and great glory" (1 Ne. 22:24). His name, Jeremiah foretold, would be "Jehovah, our Righteousness" (Jer. 23:5–6; 33:16, literal translation). "The king of Israel, even the Lord," reported Zephaniah concerning the Millennium, "is in the midst of thee" (Zeph. 3:15). And to Zechariah God said, "The Lord shall be king over all the earth: in that day shall there be one Lord, and his name one" (Zech. 14:9; see also vv. 16–17).

The New Testament also identifies Israel's millennial king as Christ, who will rule at his second coming as "King of kings, and Lord of Lords" (Rev. 19:16), sitting on "the throne of his father David: and he shall reign over the house of Jacob for ever" (Luke 1:32–33; see also Isa. 9:6–7). In modern revelation we learn that "the Lord shall be in their midst, and his glory shall be upon them, and he will be their king and their lawgiver" (D&C 45:59). As the Prophet Joseph Smith summarized, "Christ will reign personally upon the earth" when it is renewed and receives "its paradisiacal glory" (Article of Faith 10).[5] Jesus will be the "one shepherd," "even my servant David" (Ezek. 34:23). "I am the good shepherd," he proclaimed—a doctrine that is repeated in many passages (John 10:14; see also Heb. 13:20; 1 Pet. 5:4; Alma 5:38, 39, 41, 57, 60; D&C 50:44). Nephi learned from an angel that there is but "one Shepherd over all the earth" (1 Ne. 13:41), and many have testified that there will be "one fold and one shepherd" (1 Ne. 22:25; Hel. 15:13; 3 Ne. 15:17, 21; 16:3). Certainly, since the scriptures identify Jesus Christ as the *one* Shepherd and the *one* King, we need not look for another to take his place.

In the Millennium, all things will be restored to their proper place and order. Every longing for the glories of the past will be realized. Dwelling in peace and safety in its promised land, the covenant family of Israel will be ruled by its true King, the Good Shepherd Jehovah. With him ruling as Shepherd and King, it will be a day of well-being for all the Lord's people. If the time of David's rule was a golden age, then the time of Christ's millennial rule will be one of transcendent happiness and blessing.[6]

NOTES

1. The passages from Ezekiel 34 are arranged according to Ezekiel's Hebrew poetry.

2. Andrew F. Ehat and Lyndon W. Cook, eds., *The Words of Joseph Smith: The Contemporary Accounts of the Nauvoo Discourses of the Prophet Joseph* (Provo, Utah: Religious Studies Center, Brigham Young University, 1980), 331; spelling standardized where necessary for readability.

3. The idea that the millennial David is someone other than Christ seems to be a rather recent idea that may not have appeared in the Church until the second half of the twentieth century. It does not seem to be reflected either in the *Journal of Discourses* or in any general conference talks. See *Journal of Discourses*, 26 vols. (Liverpool: Latter-day Saints' Book Depot, 1854–86), 14:350–51; 15:110; 20:154; 22:83.

4. Later Israelites seem to have overlooked or forgotten David's fall and the tragedies that resulted from it in the latter part of his reign. In their tradition he always remained the ideal king.

5. Elder Orson Hyde's dedicatory prayer on the Mount of Olives in Jerusalem refers to "David," "even a descendant from the loins of ancient David," as Israel's future king (*Times and Seasons* 3, no. 11 [1 April 1842]: 740). Since the scriptures identify the millennial king as Christ, Elder Hyde's reference to "David" must be similarly understood.

6. For additional references to Christ as Israel's millennial king, see the Topical Guide in the LDS edition of the King James Bible under "Jesus Christ, Millennial Reign," and "Jesus Christ, King."

13

THE STICK OF JOSEPH AND THE STICK OF JUDAH

Ezekiel was a prophet who was born in the kingdom of Judah but was taken into Babylonian exile with others of his countrymen, probably in 597 B.C.[1] While in Babylonia, he was called to preach repentance but was warned that his listeners would be unreceptive (see Ezek. 2:3–7; 3:7). Nonetheless, he delivered the Lord's message: If the people of Jerusalem would not repent, their city would be destroyed and they, like Ezekiel and others already, would be taken from their homes to a new land. After Jerusalem's fall in 586 B.C., Ezekiel's prophecies turned from the coming destruction of his people to events of their future, especially their distant future. He foretold the day of the reunion of Israel and Judah, their return to their promised land, and the reign of their millennial king. In short, he prophesied of their restoration as God's people. Modern revelation is the key to understanding Ezekiel's prophecies, and it allows us to see their fulfillment in the latter days.

Ezekiel's vision of the uniting of the two sticks (Ezek. 37:15–28) is one of the Bible's best-known prophecies for Latter-day Saints. But most are aware only of its important secondary message, the joining of scriptural records, and not of the primary focus of the revelation—the restoration of the house of Israel with Christ as king. As the revelation begins, the Lord commands Ezekiel to take in hand two "sticks." The Hebrew word translated "stick," *'ēṣ,* has as its primary meanings "tree" and "wood."[2] The most likely meaning in this context is a piece of wood, a board. One interpretation that is well known in the Church proposes that Ezekiel envisioned a writing board called a *diptych,* which consisted of two pieces of wood hinged together to fold like the covers of a book. The inside surfaces of the boards were recessed and coated with wax, providing a convenient and reusable writing medium.[3] While this explanation is not certain, it is reasonable and could well approximate what Ezekiel saw.[4] In any case, the boards in the revelation were symbols meant to represent greater things, and thus their exact nature is not as significant as the message conveyed through them.

Ezekiel was commanded to write the following on the first board: "Belonging to Judah and the children of Israel his companions." On the second he was commanded to write: "Belonging to Joseph—the stick of Ephraim—and all the house of Israel his companions" (Ezek. 37:16, my translations). These are phrases of identification that were very commonly used in ancient Israel and Judah to designate ownership. The message is clear: one board belonged to Judah and the other to Joseph. As the revelation continued, Ezekiel was instructed to place the two boards together in one: "and they shall become one in thine hand" (Ezek. 37:17).

This revelation is one of several in which the Lord commanded Ezekiel to engage in highly symbolic actions.[5] As "visual aids," the actions were meant to convey messages of importance to the house of Israel, and they were almost always followed by explanations of their purpose and meaning. In this case the explanation follows in verses 18–28. When we add to the material provided in those verses some significant things that we learn through modern revelation, we gain a clear understanding of the truths Ezekiel taught by means of the two "sticks." As is apparent in verses 21–27, the central message of Ezekiel's revelation is the restoration of the house of Israel. For Latter-day Saints the word *restoration* usually evokes thoughts of Joseph Smith and the restoration of lost truth and authority in the latter days. But the restoration, in its greatest sense, involves much more than that. As Ezekiel reported, it includes the gathering of the dispersed of Israel (see Ezek. 37:21), their reestablishment in promised lands (see Ezek. 37:21–22, 25), the restoration of Judah and Israel into one nation (see Ezek. 37:22), the restoration of their status as a worthy covenant people before the Lord (see Ezek. 37:23–24, 26–28), and the restoration of the Lord himself to his rightful position as Israel's divine king (see Ezek. 37:22, 24–25). These constitute the central focus of Ezekiel 37 and of many other important prophecies as well. For all of these, the Lord provided a sign: the bringing together of the two inscribed pieces of wood—the "stick of Judah" and the "stick of Joseph, which is in the hand of Ephraim" (Ezek. 37:19).

Two Sacred Records

Our distinctive Latter-day Saint point of view regarding Ezekiel's sticks came in a revelation to the Prophet Joseph Smith in August 1830, in which the Lord spoke of Moroni, "whom I have sent unto you to reveal the Book of Mormon, containing the fulness of my everlasting gospel, to whom I have committed the keys of the record of the stick of Ephraim" (D&C 27:5). Ezekiel's visionary stick of Joseph in Ephraim's hand thus represents Joseph's scriptural record—the Book of Mormon. It follows, therefore, that Judah's stick represents the scriptural record of Judah—the Bible.

Ezekiel was not the only prophet who knew of the coming together of the two scriptural records. Through modern revelation we learn that almost a thousand years earlier, ancient Joseph received a revelation from which he knew of the joining of the record of his descendants with that of the tribe of Judah. This would be done under the ministry of the great latter-day seer, Joseph Smith, who would be an instrument in the Lord's hand to bring to pass the restoration of Israel. We know of this revelation from two sources—from the Book of Mormon and from the Joseph Smith Translation of the Bible. Lehi, who found the revelation on the plates of brass, considered it to be significant enough to give it special emphasis for his family. Nephi recorded it on his small plates (see 2 Ne. 3:4–24). The Lord told ancient Joseph: "Wherefore, the fruit of thy loins shall write; and the fruit of the loins of Judah shall write; and that which shall be written by the fruit of thy loins, and also that which shall be written by the fruit of the loins of Judah, shall grow together, unto the confounding of false doctrines and laying down of contentions, and establishing peace among the fruit of thy loins, and bringing them to the knowledge of their fathers in the latter days, and also to the knowledge of my covenants, saith the Lord" (2 Ne. 3:12; see also 1 Ne. 13:41; JST Gen. 50:31).

The Lord told ancient Joseph that the great latter-day seer's ministry would include "convincing them of my word, which shall have already gone forth among them" (2 Ne. 3:11; JST Gen. 50:30). As the Lord revealed in 1830 when the Church was organized, one important purpose for the coming forth of the Book of Mormon was to bear testimony of the truth of the Bible (see D&C 20:11; see also 1 Ne. 13:39–40). The coming together of the records of Joseph and Judah enables each to bear testimony of the message of the other and both together to bear testimony of the Lord and his work. In Nephi's words, "they both shall be established in one" (1 Ne. 13:41). The coming together of the two records is thus a central event in the restoration of the house of Israel. Indeed, it is an essential ingredient in the Lord's latter-day work, for the gospel message thus produced will confound false doctrine, lay down contentions, establish peace between the two estranged halves of the house of Israel, and bring them to a knowledge of God's covenants (compare Ezek. 37:22–23, 26–27). It is no wonder, then, that in Ezekiel's prophecy the bringing together of the two records—the sticks of Joseph and Judah—is the very symbol of the restoration of Israel.

Other prophets also foretold this event as the sign of Israel's restoration. The Savior himself did so when he ministered to the children of Lehi following his resurrection. While teaching them of the restoration of Israel, he spoke of the coming forth of their record, the Book of Mormon. He called it a sign: "I give unto you a sign, that ye may know the time when these things shall be about to take place—that I shall gather in, from their long dispersion, my people, O house of Israel, and shall establish again among them my Zion" (3 Ne. 21:1). The sign would be the coming forth of their record, by which both they and the Gentiles would know that they are "a remnant of the house of Jacob" (3 Ne. 21:2; see also vv. 3–6). "And when these things come to pass that thy seed shall begin to know these things—it shall be a sign unto them, that they may know that the work of the Father hath already commenced unto the fulfilling of the covenant which he hath made unto the people who are of the house of Israel" (3 Ne. 21:7). Mormon, who compiled the record of Joseph, also saw its publication as a sign of Israel's restoration: "When the Lord shall see fit, in his wisdom, that these sayings shall come unto the Gentiles according to his word, then ye may know that the covenant which the Father hath made with the children of Israel, concerning their restoration to the lands of their inheritance, is already beginning to be fulfilled" (3 Ne. 29:1; see also vv. 2–9). Because the Bible was already known when the Book of Mormon was first published in 1830, the appearance of the Book of Mormon was, to a great extent, the coming together of the two records—the sign that the reunion of the branches of Israel and their reestablishment in the covenants would soon take place. But the mere availability of the two records does not mean that their union is complete. Elder Boyd K. Packer pointed out in 1982 that the Latter-day Saint editions of the scriptures are a part of the bringing together of the sticks foreseen by Ezekiel: "The stick or record of Judah—the Old Testament and the New Testament— and the stick or record of Ephraim—the Book of Mormon, which is another testament of Jesus Christ—are now woven together in such a way that as you pore over one you are drawn to the other; as you learn from one you are enlightened by the other. They are indeed one in our hands."[6] As Latter-day Saints weave the scriptures together in their gospel study, they see the fulfillment of Ezekiel's prophecy of the unification of the records of Judah and Joseph. And they can be sure that the prophecy to which that unification points—the restoration and reunion of the two peoples— will likewise be fulfilled.

The latter-day restoration of the house of Israel, according to Ezekiel, would involve not only the gathering of the dispersed to their promised land (see Ezek. 37:21, 25) but also the reunification of the two rival nations, Israel and Judah (see Ezek. 37:22). The united monarchy of David and Solomon split into two separate countries shortly after Solomon's death (see 1 Kgs. 12), with the northern ten tribes constituting the kingdom of Israel and the tribes of Judah and Benjamin making up the kingdom of Judah. Since that time, they had been rival kingdoms with separate histories, separate ruling families, and separate destinies. Israel— which was frequently called "Joseph" or "Ephraim" in the scriptures[7]—was destroyed by the Assyrians a century and a half before Ezekiel received this revelation. Many of its people who survived the warfare were deported to other parts of the Assyrian empire (see 2 Kgs. 17:1–24), from which their descendants now have lost their identity and have become assimilated into the nations of the world. By the time of Ezekiel's revelation, Judah had been conquered by the Babylonians. Its capital city, Jerusalem, lay in ruins, as did the temple there, and much of its population had been deported to Mesopotamia (including Ezekiel) or had been scattered or directed elsewhere (including Lehi).

ONE NATION

Under these circumstances, Ezekiel's revelation of the reunification of Israel and Judah was remarkable. Like the two inscribed boards, they would be brought together again and would become "one nation . . . , and they shall be no more two nations, neither shall they be divided into two kingdoms any more at all" (Ezek. 37:22). This is a prophecy of greatest importance that still has not been fulfilled. But we know who the two nations are today, and we know what must be done before they will be brought together. Judah consists of the Jews, who, though scattered in most of the nations of the earth, still, to a large extent, have retained their identity. Aside from those who have accepted the restored gospel, they are still removed from the blessings of the covenants which the Lord established with their fathers in biblical times. Israel is The Church of Jesus Christ of Latter-day Saints, the vast majority of whose members belong (either by birth or by adoption) to the northern tribes of Ephraim and Manasseh. They have gathered to the Church from their scattered state throughout the world. The prophesied reunification of the two groups will come when the descendants of Judah accept the covenants of the gospel of Jesus Christ and join with their brothers and sisters of Israel in the Lord's Church.

Ezekiel's prophecy of the restoration of Israel's kingship is also remarkable. He used the name "David" for the messianic ruler: "And David my servant shall be king over them; and they all shall have one shepherd. . . . And my servant David shall be their prince for ever" (Ezek. 37:24–25). As we saw in chapter 12, Jesus Christ is this latter-day "David," the "king," the "shepherd," and the "prince" of Israel. In the Millennium, the time in which all of Ezekiel's promises will find their ultimate realization, he "will reign personally upon the earth," as Joseph Smith prophesied (Article of Faith 10).

The restored Israelite nation, in its several millennial locations, will be Zion, a community of faithful individuals who have overcome sin and have joined the Lord in covenants. They will be those, as Moroni wrote, "whose garments are white through the blood of the Lamb . . . , for they have been washed in the blood of the Lamb; and they are they who were scattered and gathered in from the four quarters of the earth, and from the north countries, and are partakers of the fulfilling of the covenant which God made with their father, Abraham" (Ether 13:10–11).[8] When the covenant is renewed and the relationship restored between Jehovah and his people, it will be "a covenant of peace . . . an everlasting covenant" (Ezek. 37:26). And again the Lord will affirm, "I will be their God, and they shall be my people" (Ezek. 37:27; see also v. 23).

NOTES

1. For the historical background, see Gary Lee Walker, "The Fall of the Kingdom of Judah," in Kent P. Jackson, ed., *First Kings to Malachi*, vol. 4 in Studies in Scripture series (Salt Lake City: Deseret Book, 1993), 165–77.

2. Current English-language translations render the word here in a variety of ways: "stick" (Jewish Publication Society Bible, New Revised Standard Version), "stick of wood" (New International Version), "leaf of a wooden tablet" (Revised English Bible).

3. See Keith A. Meservy, "Ezekiel's Sticks and the Gathering of Israel," *Ensign,* February 1987, 4–13. Excellent photographs of a diptych can be seen in *National Geographic,* December 1987, 730–31.

4. Meservy's writing board interpretation, which he proposed

originally in the 1970s (*Ensign,* September 1977, 22–27), is adopted in the footnote to Ezekiel 37:16 in the LDS edition of the King James Bible.

5. Some others include Ezekiel 2:9–3:4; 4:1–8, 9–17; 5:1–5, 12.

6. Packer, Conference Report, October 1982, 75; see also 73–76.

7. For Joseph, see Ezekiel 37:16, 19; Obadiah 1:18; Zechariah 10:6. For Ephraim, see Isaiah 7:2, 5, 8, 9, 17; 11:13; 17:3; Jeremiah 7:15; 31:6, 9, 18, 20; Ezekiel 37:16, 19; Hosea 4:17; 5:3, 11–14; 6:4, 10; 8:9, 11; 9:3; 10:6, 11; 11:3, 8, 9, 12; Zechariah 9:10, 13. It is likely that several other more ambiguous references to Joseph and Ephraim also refer to the entire kingdom of Israel.

8. The terms "four quarters of the earth" and "north countries" both represent the various locations throughout the earth where the house of Israel was scattered. Since north was the direction to which the deportees of Israel and Judah were taken, their return is often described as being from the north.

14

APOCALYPTIC REVELATION

Several sections of the scriptures in which visions are presented appear in a highly symbolic revelatory style called "apocalyptic."[1] Apocalyptic vision is the mode of revelation in which the observer is withdrawn from the earthly sphere with its normal circumstances of time and space and is moved, as it were, into the realm of the divine. In this realm he no longer sees things from an earthly perspective but from the perspective of the visionary sphere. Most often what he sees there cannot be described in earthly terms and can be characterized only with the use of vivid, dramatic symbols, most of which transcend our understanding of "normal" space, logic, time, and the rules of science as we know them. Several of Ezekiel's visions are excellent examples of this, as are some of Daniel's visions, much of Zechariah, and, from the New Testament, the book of Revelation. Although they lack the intense imagery of the visions of Ezekiel and Daniel, Lehi's and Nephi's visions of the tree of life exhibit apocalyptic characteristics. In those visions, Lehi and Nephi were transported into a world of symbols. It seems safe to suggest that the tree, the rod of iron, the great building, and the other things they saw never actually existed except as symbols in the vision to teach what the Lord wants us to learn (see 1 Ne. 8–14).[2]

Apocalyptic vision is characterized by what is called "dualism," the idea of the universal struggle between the forces of evil and good. In the here and now, the forces of evil often prevail. But there will be an end-of-the-world time in which the forces of good—God and his chosen Saints—will triumph over the forces of evil—Satan and his hosts. In apocalyptic revelation, the victory of right over wrong does not take place as a result of the natural flow of history. Instead, there is a dramatic break with the past, as God and his forces stop the course of human events to defeat the powers of darkness and bring the world into the final age of peace and glory. God's ultimate victory is sure; it is predetermined. This kind of revelation is highly typological—it abounds in vivid symbols, or "types." A type is a symbol that serves as a pattern, frequently representing more than one specific thing, event, or circumstance. Often types represent whole categories. For example, the scenes depicted in the Tree of Life vision did not represent a specific event in the experience of Lehi's family but a lifelong process by which they, and millions of others, choose to follow either God or the ways of the world. Apocalyptic prophecies are "fulfilled" whenever the categories that are depicted exist. In other words, they can be "fulfilled" more than once and with different individuals or nations involved. At the same time, however, they point to a grand and *ultimate* fulfillment, on a universal scale, in a last-days setting.

The symbolism in apocalyptic vision is thus much different from metaphor, the literary imagery that is used so abundantly throughout the Old Testament. A metaphor is a word or group of words used in place of something else to suggest a likeness between them: Israel is a tree that bears fruit, the prophet is a pillar, we drink a bitter cup of sorrow, one's testimony is built on a solid foundation, and we are sheep gone astray. Metaphor is intended to be understood, by bringing to mind comparisons with well-known images. For the most part it is easily comprehended by those who are familiar with the culture, history, language, geography, and social circumstances in which the scripture originated.[3] Apocalyptic vision, in contrast, is meant to be understood fully only with the help of more revelation. Joseph Smith taught this principle when he said: "When the prophets speak of seeing beasts in their visions, they saw the images—types to represent certain things. And at the same time they received the interpretation as to what those images or types were designed to represent. I make this broad declaration, that where God ever gives a vision of an image, or beast, or figure of any kind, he always holds himself responsible to give a revelation or interpretation of the meaning thereof, otherwise we are not responsible or accountable for our belief in it. Don't be afraid of being damned for not knowing the meaning of a vision or figure where God has not given a revelation or interpretation on the subject."[4] In section 77 of the Doctrine and Covenants, for example, we have the revelation needed to understand the symbols in important passages of John's Apocalypse. But often the additional revelation comes in the form of an angelic interpreter. Nephi was accompanied through the symbolic world of the tree of life vision by a heavenly messenger, who translated its symbols for him (see 1 Ne. 8–14). Modern readers can understand its meaning because of the interpretation the messenger provided. For several other apocalyptic visions, however, the Lord has not yet seen fit to provide an interpretation in the scriptures. Thus we must read them with caution and recognize that we will not fully understand them until the Lord makes their meaning known.

As in all our study of the Bible, a knowledge of modern revelation is indispensable. Through the revelations and translations of Joseph Smith, the Lord has given us many keys to help us understand individual Bible passages. But more important still, he has revealed in the last days the big picture of his eternal plan. Knowing who we are, where we came from, and what God does and will yet do for us will open to our understanding many of the revelations of the ancient prophets.

NOTES

1. Since definitions of apocalyptic literature vary, no universally accepted list exists. D. S. Russell includes only the book of Daniel from the Old Testament in his list of fully developed apocalyptic literature; see *The Method and Message of Jewish Apocalyptic* (Philadelphia: Westminster, 1976), 36–39. He includes Ezekiel 38–39, Zechariah, Joel 3, and Isaiah 24–27 in a transitional category that later developed into full apocalyptic.

2. The apocalyptic nature of the latter part of the vision is even more apparent. See Stephen E. Robinson, "Early Christianity and 1 Nephi 13–14," in *First Nephi: The Doctrinal Foundation,* ed. Monte S. Nyman and Charles D. Tate (Provo, Utah: Religious Studies Center, Brigham Young University, 1988), 177–91.

3. As Nephi wrote, the Jews could understand the writings of their prophets because they were intimately familiar with these things (see 2 Ne. 25:5–6). See chapter 8 in the present volume.

4. Andrew F. Ehat and Lyndon W. Cook, eds., *The Words of Joseph Smith: The Contemporary Accounts of the Nauvoo Discourses of the Prophet Joseph* (Provo, Utah: Religious Studies Center, Brigham Young University, 1980), 185; punctuation and spelling standardized where necessary for readability.

15

ARMAGEDDON

The Bible foretells latter-day events of great importance. But left to the Bible alone, many Christians have adopted beliefs that cannot be sustained in the light of the revelations to the Prophet Joseph Smith. The dramatic future scene invoked through the ominous-sounding word *Armageddon* is of particular interest to some. Through close examination of the scriptural sources, especially in modern revelation, we are able to put this word in context and understand it correctly. For the following thoughts, the discussion in chapter 14 is intended to be a helpful introduction.

ARMAGEDDON IN THE BIBLE

The word *Armageddon* is not found in the Old Testament, but it is frequently associated with Old Testament prophecy. It appears only one time in the scriptures, in John's vision in the book of Revelation (Rev. 16:16). It is not found in the Book of Mormon, the Doctrine and Covenants, or the Pearl of Great Price. Just as significantly, it is not found in any of the recorded teachings or writings of the Prophet Joseph Smith. Nor is any battle found in modern revelation which bears that name. It is perhaps

125

surprising, therefore, that the "Battle of Armageddon" looms so large in the belief of some Latter-day Saints, who see it as a great battle that will be raging when the Second Coming takes place. Yet the "Battle of Armageddon" is not a scriptural term but a concept that some Latter-day Saints have borrowed from other Christians. The fact that *Armageddon* is not found in modern revelation is important, because modern revelation, not the Bible, is the source of Latter-day Saint doctrine, and modern revelation is the means by which we understand what is written in the Bible.

Many commentators have identified the word *Armageddon* with the ancient Holy Land site of Megiddo, suggesting that the name comes from *har* (Hebrew, "mountain") and Megiddo, that is, "Mt. Megiddo."[1] This interpretation is an educated guess, an attempt to make sense out of an enigmatic word. It may be true, but it is linguistically and historically uncertain. For one thing, no ancient text, including the Bible, ever speaks of a "Mt. Megiddo," and the ancient place Megiddo was not a mountain but a city. In Revelation 16:16, John uses *Armageddon* (Greek *Harmagedōn*) in a prophecy that is full of apocalyptic images that are very difficult to interpret. In the midst of those images, he sees "the spirits of devils, working miracles, which go forth unto the kings of the earth and of the whole world, to gather them to the battle of that great day of God Almighty. . . . And he gathered them together into a place called in the Hebrew tongue Armageddon" (Rev. 16:14, 16). The verses that follow speak of calamitous destruction in dramatic and fearsome language. This is clearly apocalyptic revelation, with vivid images meant to highlight the universal conflict between good and evil (see chapter 14 of this volume). The book of Revelation sometimes draws vocabulary from Old Testament passages, including place names, to serve as apocalyptic types—such as *Gog, Magog, Egypt, Sodom,* and *Babylon.*[2] The suggestion is that Megiddo is being used the same way in Revelation 16, because battles took place there and thus its name would be associated with dramatic warfare. This is not impossible, because battles fought near there are mentioned in the Bible (see Judg. 5:19; 2 Chron. 35:22). But Megiddo and the nearby battles play only a minor role in the Bible, and in all likelihood other places would have been more successful in invoking images of dramatic warfare in the minds of John's readers. But in apocalyptic prophecy, details like this are not important, and the general mood and feeling brought forth by the word *Armageddon,* whatever its source, was likely sufficient to communicate to John's readers that something ominous was to happen in the last days. In any case, it is not likely that the place itself is prophetically significant, because the word is used typologically in an apocalyptic context, and because no other scripture suggests a future importance for that location or any future battle that will take place there.

The context in which the word *Armageddon* is used in Revelation 16 is not a war between nations at all. God gathers the armies together (see Rev. 16:16), but the text gives no hint that they are gathered to fight against each other. Instead, this is God's own war against the wicked world, "the battle of that great day of God Almighty" (Rev. 16:14). After the nations are assembled, a voice from "the temple of heaven" announces, "It is done." Then the slaughter begins, and calamity follows calamity as God erases wickedness from the earth: thunders, lightnings, an earthquake, ruined cities, moving islands, leveled mountains, and sixty-pound hailstones. Note that these are all natural causes, not man-made events. Babylon, the very personification of the world's pride and wickedness, receives her cup full of "the wine of the fierceness of [God's] wrath" (Rev. 16:17–21). In John's following chapter, which develops the personification of Babylon further, we learn that her minions "make war with the Lamb." But "the Lamb shall overcome them: for he is Lord of lords, and King of kings" (Rev. 17:14). In the Old Testament, we have other witnesses of the same event. For example, the prophet Joel depicted the same scene in similar words, with God bringing the nations together to pass judgment on them (see Joel 3:1–16). In one passage, Joel calls the place "the valley of Jehoshaphat," meaning "the Lord judges" (Joel 3:2).[3] Elsewhere he calls it "the valley of decision" (Joel 3:14). Like the battle at Armageddon, Joel's battle is the scene in which God brings his recompense against the world. The Lord revealed to the Prophet Joseph Smith that when Christ returns, he will be "red in his apparel." He will say, "I have . . . brought judgment upon all people; and none were with me; and I have trampled them in my fury, and I did tread upon them in mine anger, and their blood have I sprinkled upon my garments, and stained all my raiment; for this was the day of vengeance which was in my heart" (D&C 133:48, 50–51). That battle—with its apocalyptic locations at Armageddon and the valleys of Jehoshaphat and Decision—represents God's cleansing of the world and the removal of wickedness and wicked people, necessary steps in the preparation of the earth for the Savior's second coming. That is the only context in which the scriptures foretell a battle associated with the word *Armageddon.* Thus it is not likely that the names of the places have any real geographical meaning, representing as they do the universal scene of God's punishing and purifying.

ARMAGEDDON, WAR, AND JERUSALEM

We have been concerned with the word *Armageddon* itself and with the only context in the scriptures in which it is used. But most often, commentators remove the word from that context and apply it to other settings to mean other things. Thus the "battle of Armageddon" is a name some have given to worldwide warfare at the time of the Second Coming, or to a battle at Jerusalem when Jesus appears, or to both. When Armageddon is discussed, it is usually in association with apocalyptic Old Testament prophecies that are difficult to understand and that require both content and context from modern revelation. These include Ezekiel's prophecy of "Gog" of the land of "Magog" (see Ezek. 38–39), which points to the Lord's deliverance of the faithful from Satan's quest to destroy their souls, and the visions of Joel, which foretell in symbolic ways the Lord's overflowing scourges to purify the earth (see Joel 1:1–2:11) and his judgments against the wickedness of the world (see Joel 3:1–16). Also cited is a series of prophecies in the book of Zechariah, some of which foretell end-time events with vivid, apocalyptic battle images. In one of Zechariah's battle prophecies, Jerusalem is characterized as a stone too heavy to be moved out of its place and its people as a torch among kindling wood. Those who come to battle against it will be defeated and destroyed, because the Lord will defend his people (see Zech. 12:1–9). Another scene shows two-thirds of the people of the land perishing and a third surviving. That third, in turn, will be tried in the refiner's fire, and they will be acknowledged as the Lord's people (see Zech. 13:7–9). In another battle prophecy (Zech. 14:1–5), Zechariah depicts the nations attacking Jerusalem and overpowering and conquering it. The victory will be short-lived, however, because Jehovah himself will intervene and fight. "Then shall the Lord go forth, and fight against those nations, as when he fought in the day of battle" (Zech. 14:3). He will stand on the Mount of Olives, which will divide in two, and the inhabitants of Jerusalem will flee to safety. In passages like these, it is not always clear what names like *Jerusalem* and *Israel* represent. Perhaps the apocalyptic vision is intended to draw our thoughts beyond the confines of the Holy City, to look for a fulfillment of the prophecy on a more universal scale. Perhaps they represent the Lord's Saints wherever they may be, scattered among the people of the world. Perhaps other fulfillments are intended.

It is interesting to observe that in none of the biblical

prophecies noted do we have two armies gathered to fight against each other. Instead, the combatants are the world and the Lord. The nations wage war against Israel, but Israel is not depicted as fighting. It is the Lord who fights his people's battles, and he is always victorious.[4]

Between Zechariah's battle visions are other inspired words of importance. In beautiful language, the Lord depicts a dramatic scene of reconciliation between him and his own family and nation: "I will pour upon the house of David, and upon the inhabitants of Jerusalem, the spirit of grace and of supplications: and they shall look upon me whom they have pierced, and they shall mourn for him, as one mourneth for his only son, and shall be in bitterness for him, as one that is in bitterness for his first-born." This will be followed by much sadness among all the families of the land (Zech. 12:10; see also vv. 11–14). Our Latter-day Saint interpretation comes from a revelation to Joseph Smith: "And then shall the Jews look upon me and say: What are these wounds in thine hands and in thy feet? Then shall they know that I am the Lord; for I will say unto them: These wounds are the wounds with which I was wounded in the house of my friends. I am he who was lifted up. I am Jesus that was crucified. I am the Son of God. And then shall they weep because of their iniquities; then shall they lament because they persecuted their king" (D&C 45:51–53).[5]

What does modern revelation teach us about warfare in the future and at Jerusalem specifically? In the Book of Mormon, we have a history of events that preceded Jesus' coming to ancient America following his resurrection. President Ezra Taft Benson taught, "The record of the Nephite history just prior to the Savior's visit reveals many parallels to our own day as we antici-pate the Savior's second coming."[6] That record shows the follow-ing developments in the thirty-four years before Christ's appearing: persecution of righteous Saints, signs from heaven, mass conversion, peace, insurrection, apostasy (see 3 Ne. 1), disbelief, preaching and prophesying, insurrection, warfare (see 3 Ne. 2), repentance among the Lord's people (see 3 Ne. 3), war (see 3 Ne. 4), repentance among the Lord's people (see 3 Ne. 5), restoration of society following war, prosperity, pride because of riches, dissolution of the Church, wickedness, preaching of repentance, murder of prophets, insurrection (see 3 Ne. 6), dissolution of government and society into tribes and families, apostasy among the Lord's people, preaching of repentance (see 3 Ne. 7), and righteous Saints looking for the signs of Christ's coming (see 3 Ne. 8:3). Many of these events characterize Nephite and Lamanite society through much of their history, yet it appears that the cycles occurred at a much-quickened pace in the generation before Jesus' coming. Next came the judgments of God to cleanse the land of wickedness—an awesome three-hour display of divine power expressed through the forces of nature (see 3 Ne. 8:19): a great storm, tempest, terrible thunder, exceedingly sharp lightnings, burning cities, sinking cities, cities buried under the earth, great and terrible destruction, quaking of the earth, and thick darkness (see 3 Ne. 8).

If these chapters in the Book of Mormon show how things will be when Jesus comes to the world in glory, then we can anticipate continued opposition to the Lord's work and yet continued conversion and growth of the Church. We can look forward to great spiritual strength among Latter-day Saints as well as many of them falling prey to sin. And we can anticipate warfare as well as a time of rapid decline and disintegration of the institutions of society. Faithful Latter-day Saints—and certainly honorable Christians of other denominations—will be "looking forth for the great day of the Lord to come, even for the signs of the coming of the Son of Man" (D&C 45:39). Finally, the chaos of the world will be interrupted by the Lord's dramatic intervention to bring judgment upon humankind—judgment and cleansing to prepare the earth for Christ's millennial reign.

In the Doctrine and Covenants and the Pearl of Great Price, we learn that there will indeed be wars in the latter days. Yet perhaps surprisingly, warfare is not mentioned frequently nor with special emphasis in the latter-day revelations. In the Doctrine and Covenants, we learn that Jesus told his ancient apostles of "wars and rumors of wars, and the whole earth shall be in commotion," and men will "take up the sword, one against another, and they will kill one another" (D&C 45:26, 33). This prophecy foretells events after the days of the ancient apostles. Both verses cited (D&C 45:26, 33) appear *before* references to the time of the Restoration (see D&C 45:28–29, 34–36), yet the intended chronology is not certain. Peace will be "taken from the earth, and the devil shall have power over his own dominion" (D&C 1:35). God "decreed wars upon the face of the earth, and the wicked shall slay the wicked" (D&C 63:33; see also Morm. 4:5), and war will be "poured out upon all nations" (D&C 87:2; see also JS–H 1:45). Sadly, we need not look to a future generation for the fulfillment of these prophecies, for everything they describe matches well the world in which we live today and the world as it has been, at least from time to time, in recent history. But the Lord also foretold a day, after the New Jerusalem will be built, when its inhabitants "shall be the only people that shall not be at war one with another. And it shall be said among the wicked: Let us not go up to battle against Zion, for the inhabitants of Zion are terrible; wherefore we cannot stand" (D&C 45:69–70; see also vv. 66–68, 71). The most systematic end-time prophecy in modern revelation is Joseph Smith–Matthew, the Prophet's inspired translation of Matthew 24 in the Pearl of Great Price (see JS–M 1:21–55). In it, Jesus twice tells his latter-day elect that they will "hear of wars, and rumors of wars." "For nation shall rise against nation, and kingdom against kingdom" (JS–M 1:23, 28–29). Again, events of our own time fit these descriptions well, yet that is all Jesus had to say about warfare in this important prophecy of last-days events. Notably, in these passages Jesus said to his Saints only that they would *hear* of these wars and rumors of wars (see JS–M 1:23, 28).

Nowhere in this revelation, nor anywhere else in modern scripture, is there mention of a battle happening at Jerusalem when the Second Coming takes place. No battle is mentioned at the time Jesus sets his foot on the Mount of Olives, though other dramatic events are foretold, including signs and wonders, darkening of the sun and the moon, resurrection of faithful Saints, trembling of the earth, and other calamities (see D&C 45:40–50). Nor is warfare mentioned when the Savior shows his wounded hands and feet to the Jews (see D&C 45:51–53). Nor is warfare mentioned when the two prophets preach and die in Jerusalem (see D&C 77:15–16; see also Rev. 11:1–12). One point of emphasis in Joseph Smith–Matthew is that when Jesus' second coming takes place, men and women will be going about their normal affairs. Like the people in the days of Noah, they will be oblivious to the calamity about to overtake them. Hence the warning, "Watch, therefore, for you know not at what hour your Lord doth come" (D&C 45:46; see also vv. 38–44, 47–48).

Notes

1. This is the interpretation adopted in the Bible Dictionary of the LDS edition of the King James Bible, 614. See the discussion in Jon Paulien, "Armageddon," in *Anchor Bible Dictionary,* ed. David Noel Freedman (New York: Doubleday, 1992), 1:394–95.

2. E.g., Revelation 11:8; 16:16; 17:5; 20:8.

3. Predictably for this apocalyptic image, a "valley of Jehoshaphat" is otherwise unknown in the Bible or in ancient geography. Medieval tradition, with no scriptural basis, equated it with Jerusalem's Kidron Valley. See Cecil Roth, ed., *Encyclopedia Judaica* (Jerusalem: Keter, 1971), 9:1327–28.

4. In the vision in Zechariah 14:12–15, which seems to be out of

context here, utter chaos and degradation reign: plagues among people and animals, rotting flesh, panic, and each individual attacking and fighting his neighbor.

5. In its present form, Zechariah 13:2–6 foretells the end of false prophecy in Israel, in which even the parents of a false prophet will not hesitate to attempt to execute him. But because Jesus' words in Doctrine and Covenants 45:51–52 seem to draw vocabulary from that Zechariah passage, likely in its original form it was clearer, unembellished, and in harmony with Jesus' words in the revelation to Joseph Smith.

6. Ezra Taft Benson, *A Witness and a Warning: A Modern-day Prophet Testifies of the Book of Mormon* (Salt Lake City: Deseret Book, 1988), 37.

16

GOG AND MAGOG

In one extended passage in the Old Testament and in one brief mention in the New Testament, the words *Gog* and *Magog* serve to invoke images of apocalyptic, end-time warfare. We shall examine those passages here (see chapter 14 in this volume for an introduction).

GOG AND MAGOG IN EZEKIEL

Ezekiel 38–39 contains a vision that exhibits some important traits of apocalyptic revelation. It depicts an invasion of "Israel" by a foreign power called "Gog" of the land of "Magog," the "chief prince of Meshech and Tubal" (Ezek. 38:2). Gog and his forces will attack the "mountains of Israel," whose people will have been "brought forth out of the nations" (Ezek. 38:8). Like "a cloud to cover the land," Gog and his allies—"a great company, and a mighty army"—will advance on the Lord's people (Ezek. 38:15–16). But the Lord will not allow them to succeed. With earthquake, sword, pestilence, blood, rain, hailstones, fire, and brimstone, the Lord will intervene to stop Gog's attack; he and his armies will be slaughtered (see Ezek. 38:19–39:8). So massive will be Gog's armies, and so thorough their defeat, that for seven years the people of Israel will gather the weapons of their defeated enemies and use them for fuel. Their corpses will be so abundant that it will take seven months to bury them. Even after that, individuals will be employed to go through the land to find the bodies not yet buried (see Ezek. 39:9–16). Next is depicted a huge feast, at which birds and animals will gorge themselves on the blood and flesh of the slain (see Ezek. 39:17–20; see also D&C 29:20).

Apocalyptic elements are readily apparent in this vision, suggesting that it is an apocalyptic scene and not a transcript of one specific future event. The latter-day setting of the prophecy seems clear. The Lord's people are called "Israel," and they have been "gathered out of many people" and "brought forth out of the nations" (Ezek. 38:8). Israel here seems to represent neither a political entity nor a geographical location but the Lord's people wherever they may be. Israel, after all, is the family name of the Lord's Saints, the members of his Church who have gathered to the covenants of his gospel throughout the earth. In the symbolic vision, Gog, coming with vast armies from distant unknown lands, sets as his goal the devastation and plunder of the Lord's people. In apocalyptic fashion, the figure "Gog" here probably does not represent a real person or nation who will attack the Saints with military force but the powers of evil that are arrayed against the Saints, manifested in many ways, many places, and many times. Satan is the very embodiment of this evil and the archenemy of the Lord and his followers. As the vision depicts, the forces of evil will not be allowed to prevail. With a mighty act so characteristic of apocalyptic scenes, the Lord himself will intervene to put an end to evil and its consequences.

When will this prophecy be fulfilled? All around us, we can see evidence that the battle is already raging today. Although apocalyptic typology often represents entire categories rather than specific individuals or events, there are enough close parallels between this prophecy and others that the timeframe for its fulfillment seems apparent. The key to understanding Ezekiel's vision is to turn to modern revelation, where there is a clearer view of the last days and of the Lord's people in that period. In the time in which we now live, the gathering of the house of Israel and the establishment of Zion have commenced. Satan's forces are engaged in relentless battle against individual Saints and the Church. As other scriptures teach us, their efforts will increase in intensity as the coming of Christ draws near (see 1 Ne. 14:11–14; JS–M 1:30). Like the hosts of Gog, however, they will not succeed in their efforts to destroy the Lord's Church. Instead, wickedness will be wiped from the earth in preparation for his coming in glory, which will usher in a thousand-year era of millennial peace.

The Book of Mormon prophet Nephi recorded a revelation that parallels Ezekiel's prophecy in many ways, describing the same effort of Satan and his followers to destroy the latter-day Saints (see 1 Ne. 14:11–17). Whereas Ezekiel's vision used the image of a mysterious "Gog" from the equally mysterious land of "Magog," Nephi's vision used the image of a "great whore"—"the mother of abominations," "the mother of harlots"—to represent the same things that Ezekiel foretold. As Nephi described it, the Church will be found "upon all the face of the earth" (1 Ne. 14:12). The forces of evil will muster their resources "among all the nations of the Gentiles" in order to "fight against the Lamb of God" (1 Ne. 14:13). But "the power of the Lamb of God" will descend on the Saints throughout the world, and they will be "armed with righteousness and with the power of God in great glory" (1 Ne. 14:14). In his wrath, the Lord will punish the enemies of his people by subjecting them to "wars and rumors of wars among all the nations and kindreds of the earth" (1 Ne. 14:15; see also v. 16). Nephi's vision in 1 Nephi 14 is thus an additional witness for what Ezekiel foretold. But more important, it enables us to understand Ezekiel's message. Additional insight from modern revelation is provided in a Doctrine and Covenants passage describing the destruction of the wicked prior to the Second Coming: "And the great and abominable church, which is the whore of all the earth, shall be cast down by devouring fire, according as it is spoken by the mouth of Ezekiel the prophet, who spoke of these things, which have not come to pass but surely must, as I live, for abominations shall not reign" (D&C 29:21). This passage shows that Nephi and Ezekiel were fore-telling the same latter-day conflict—the assault of the powers of evil against the Lord's Saints, and the destruction of those pow-ers by the hand of God.[1]

Almost all Old Testament prophecy of the future focuses on four key latter-day events: the restoration of the house of Israel, the destruction of wickedness, the coming of the Lord, and the Millennium. It should not surprise us, then, if those are the very themes alluded to by Ezekiel in the apocalyptic vision of "Gog" of "the land of Magog." The emphasis is on the efforts of the adver-sary to overcome the Saints, followed by his destruction and the end of his evil works when the Lord intervenes to save his people. Ezekiel's conclusion bears testimony to these truths: "Now will I bring again the captivity of Jacob, and have mercy upon the whole house of Israel. . . . I have gathered them unto their own land, and have left none of them any more [in captivity]. Neither will I hide my face any more from them: for I have poured out my spirit upon the house of Israel, saith the Lord God" (Ezek. 39:25–29).

GOG AND MAGOG—
AFTER THE MILLENNIUM

One New Testament passage uses the words *Gog* and *Magog* in a context different from that of Ezekiel's prophecy. In the book of Revelation, John uses the words in his apocalyptic prophecy of a great conflict at the end of the Millennium. In Revelation 20:7–10, he writes of those whom Satan will induce to rebel against God in the adversary's final effort to destroy God's work. This will take place following his release from a thousand years of imprisonment. The forces of wickedness attack Zion, but God intervenes with fire from heaven that devours them. Satan is then "cast into the lake of fire and brimstone" (compare Jacob 5:76–77). In the prophecy, the words "Gog and Magog" are interjected almost as an exclamation. They serve either to characterize those who follow Satan's rebellion or to invoke the image of the rebellion foreseen in Ezekiel 38–39. In either case, these are typical apocalyptic images, and they reflect the vocabulary of Ezekiel's vision.

For Latter-day Saints, it is this postmillennial battle that usually comes to mind with the words *Gog* and *Magog*—not the premillennial conflict foreseen by Ezekiel.[2] Indeed, Joseph Smith stated that "the battle of Gog and Magog will be after the millennium."[3] The words *Gog* and *Magog* are not found in modern scripture, but modern revelation does enlighten us regarding the battle that John foresaw. In a revelation to Joseph Smith, we learn that "Satan shall be bound, . . . and shall not be loosed for the space of a thousand years." But when he is loosed, "for a little season," he will "gather together his armies. And Michael, the seventh angel, even the archangel, shall gather together his armies, even the hosts of heaven. And the devil shall gather together his armies; even the hosts of hell, and shall come up to battle against Michael and his armies. And then cometh the battle of the great God; and the devil and his armies shall be cast away into their own place, that they shall not have power over the saints any more at all" (D&C 88:110–14).

NOTES

1. Footnotes at Doctrine and Covenants 29:20–21 identify Ezekiel 38–39 as the prophecy referred to in this revelation. Though the wording is

not exactly the same, the identification is certainly correct, because it is the closest thing in Ezekiel to the content of Doctrine and Covenants 29:21.

2. See "Gog" in the Bible Dictionary, LDS edition of the King James Bible, 682.

3. Joseph Smith, *History of The Church of Jesus Christ of Latter-day Saints,* ed. B. H. Roberts, 2d ed. rev., 7 vols. (Salt Lake City: The Church of Jesus Christ of Latter-day Saints, 1932–51), 5:298.

17

A MILLENNIAL TEMPLE
IN JERUSALEM

While in Babylonia, the prophet Ezekiel had a dramatic apocalyptic vision in which he saw a great future temple, complete with its sacrifices and priestly officiators (see Ezek. 40–48). The visionary temple was in a new and glorified Jerusalem in his homeland of Judah, from which he had been taken captive a quarter of a century earlier. With all that he had witnessed of wickedness, destruction, deportation, and exile, we can imagine his happiness at receiving the message of the restoration of the house of Israel, its temple, and its holy city.

The great temple vision is like nothing else in the Old Testament. Its apocalyptic nature is evident. As we learn from the introductory verses, Ezekiel was transported "in the visions of God" from Babylonia to a "very high mountain" which overlooked Jerusalem and its temple to the south (Ezek. 40:2). There he was met by a man whose appearance was like bronze, who accompanied him and guided him through the vision. These elements of the revelation—transported in vision, placed on a very high mountain, nonexistent mountain north of the temple, strange angelic guide—are recognizable characteristics of apocalyptic literature. Apocalyptic visions are characterized by the use of vivid symbolic scenes that can be comprehended fully only with the

141

help of additional revelations (see chapter 14 in this volume). Thus more needs to be made known concerning this vision before we can understand all its symbols. Still, its general scene of a renewed house of Israel in a renewed promised land is clear, and modern revelation supplies the doctrinal context in which the vision's message can be understood.

A GUIDED TOUR

In the vision, Ezekiel's guide gave the prophet a detailed tour of a temple in Jerusalem, including all its surrounding structures. The guide carried with him a measuring stick with which precise measurements were provided throughout the vision (compare Rev. 21:9–10, 15–17). Ezekiel saw the area from the east gate to the outer court, the north and south gates, the gates to the inner court, rooms for the preparation of sacrifices, rooms for the priests, and the temple itself (see Ezek. 40:5–42:20). He was next brought to the gate facing east, from which he saw the glory of God approaching the temple. With radiant light and the roar of rushing waters, the glory of the Lord entered through the gate where the prophet stood and filled the Lord's house with its splendor (see Ezek. 43:1–5; 44:4). It was almost two decades earlier that Ezekiel had experienced a similar apocalyptic vision in which he saw God's glory at the temple, but then the glory was departing from it (see Ezek. 9:3; 10:18–19; 11:22–23). In that early vision, an angelic guide showed him the temple in its time of wickedness, with symbolic figures and actions that represented its apostasy and the evil works that were done in it (see Ezek. 8–11). Now, years later and following the destruction of the temple and the exile of the Jews, he saw in striking symbols a vision of the temple in a future purified state. Whereas his first temple vision represented all that was corrupt and degenerate about Israel's relationship with God, his later visionary temple represents all that will be holy and glorious about that relationship when the house of Israel is purified.

The next stop in Ezekiel's visionary tour was at the altar, where he was given instructions for the direction of the priests in their sacrifices (see Ezek. 43:13–27). He learned of the roles of the priests and the Levites in the temple. Only the "sons of Zadok," the family of the high priests, would be allowed to enter the sanctuary (see Ezek. 44:15–16).[1] Through their actions and their appearance, they would teach the Lord's people the difference between the "holy" and the "profane" and "the unclean and the clean" (Ezek. 44:23). The prophet learned, in some detail, of the offerings and holy days that would be observed in the temple. Everything was to be administered according to a prescribed plan (see Ezek. 45:13–46:23).

A new scene of the vision opened as Ezekiel's guide took him to the entrance of the temple, from which he saw water flowing from under the threshold toward the east. He and his guide followed the flow of water and measured its depth along the way. A thousand cubits from the source it was ankle deep, farther still it was knee deep, then it was up to his waist, and then it was a river, deep enough to swim in (see Ezek. 47:1–5). The water continued its flow to the Dead Sea, which became a freshwater lake on contact with the miraculous river from the temple. Ezekiel saw that swarms of living things would live wherever the river flows, and varieties of fish would inhabit the lake which had once been hostile to life (see Ezek. 47:6–10). Fruit trees of all kinds would adorn the banks of the river. "Their leaves will not wither, nor will their fruit fail. Every month they will bear, because the water from the sanctuary flows to them. Their fruit will serve for food and their leaves for healing" (Ezek. 47:12, New International Version).

The next part of Ezekiel's vision has its focus on the division of the land among the tribes (see Ezek. 47:13–48:29). All thirteen of the tribes are mentioned, and each would receive an inheritance, including Levi, which in Old Testament times did not receive territory but was settled in special cities among the other tribes. Even non-Israelites would receive an inheritance. Those who would dwell among the children of Israel would be considered as native-born Israelites and would receive an inheritance among them (see Ezek. 47:21–23).

MILLENNIAL JERUSALEM

Ezekiel's vision represents the millennial condition of the house of Israel, in which the covenant people will enjoy the blessings of their promised land, their Holy City, and their temple. The centerpiece of the vision is the house of God. In apocalyptic visions, symbols are not meant to provide a literal portrayal but to characterize or idealize. It seems that such is the case with this vision. It depicts the future glories of Israel's restoration in the most idealized images. Everything about the millennial day—including the land, the city, and the temple—would exceed by far the best of what had existed in earlier times. But the vision was limited by the level of doctrinal understanding of its readers, who were still under the law of Moses without a comprehension of the gospel of Christ and still rejected the words of living prophets, as is so evident in the book of Ezekiel. Thus the vision showed a temple of the law of Moses, patterned after the temples of ancient Israel. Officiating in it was the Aaronic Priesthood, as in biblical times (see Ezek. 43:13–27; 44:10–31), and burnt offerings, sin offerings, and fellowship ("peace") offerings are depicted (see Ezek. 43:18–27). But the scriptures make it clear that the law of Moses and its sacrifices were ended with the atonement of Christ (see Alma 34:13–14; Heb. 10:18), and so it does not seem reasonable that a temple for the performance of Mosaic animal offerings will ever again be built, especially during the Millennium when there will be no death (see chapter 21 in this volume for further exploration of this matter).[2] Future temples, both before and after the Second Coming, will undoubtedly be similar to those with which we are familiar in the Church now, in which ordinances of the Melchizedek Priesthood will be performed for the living and the dead. Ezekiel's vision portrayed the future temple by means of familiar Old Testament temple images because his readers would not have recognized or comprehended a temple like ours today. The Lord communicates with people in their own language and according to their level of understanding (see D&C 1:24), and in this vision he taught ancient Jews of millennial things by using images drawn from their own time and experience. The design, purpose, and ordinances of modern temples would have made no sense to them, just as they make no sense to Jews and other Christians today. Clearly, the real millennial temple will be much different from its visionary symbol. In it, worthy Saints will enter into covenants and participate in sacred ordinances—all designed to help them prepare to enter the presence of God in the highest degree of glory.

Who will build this temple, and when? And where will it stand? Some have suggested that Ezekiel foresaw Jews in the Holy Land building an Old Testament temple independently of the Church of Jesus Christ and without a knowledge of his gospel. But if they did, it would not be in fulfillment of prophecy or according to divine plan, because the keys of temple building are found only in The Church of Jesus Christ of Latter-day Saints (see D&C 110:13–16).[3] Moreover, the keys of the Aaronic Priesthood—the authority that presided over the ancient Israelite temples—are no longer found in Judaism but only in the Church (see JS–H 1:68–72). Ezekiel's immediate ministry was to Jews recently exiled from their homeland, who had witnessed the destruction of their kingdom, their city, and their temple. His prophecy, appropriately, has its focus in the restoration of Judah and Jerusalem. At some future time, a temple will be built in that city, yet whether it will stand on the same spot as the ancient temples does not seem to be important. What is important is the fact that one day there will be enough of the Lord's faithful covenant people in Jerusalem to have a house of God in their midst. Ezekiel's images point to a day when Israel will be gathered and its people sanctified—conditions that do not exist now but will prevail in the Millennium. While it appears that Ezekiel's temple vision will be fulfilled to its greatest extent then, there is nothing in the scriptures to preclude a sufficient population of Latter-day Saints in Jerusalem to build a temple there prior to Jesus' coming. Whether before or after the beginning of the Millennium, those who will participate in the construction and service of the Lord's house will include the Latter-day Saints who live in that area—Jews who will have gathered again to the covenants by joining the Savior's Church, Arabs who will have done likewise, and other Saints who will dwell among them.[4]

In Ezekiel's earlier vision, he witnessed the glory of the Lord leaving the temple, which had become unworthy of the divine presence (see Ezek. 10:18–19; 11:22–23). In this vision of millennial things he saw it return, this time to usher in a thousand years of Christ's reign (see Ezek. 43:1–5; 44:4). Holiness and glory will be the watchwords in that day, for they will fill the earth and characterize all that is done in it. As Zechariah foretold, even the most mundane things like pots and pans and bells on horses will be inscribed with "HOLINESS UNTO THE LORD" (Zech. 14:20–21), just as our temples are today. The inhabitants of the once-and-again Holy City will be those who "have been washed in the blood of the Lamb; and they are they who were scattered and gathered in from the four quarters of the earth, and from the north countries, and are partakers of the fulfilling of the covenant which God made with their father, Abraham" (Ether 13:11). "For the Lord shall be in their midst, and his glory shall be upon them, and he will be their king and their lawgiver" (D&C 45:59). We look forward with anticipation to the glorious Millennium and hope to be worthy to be citizens of Zion then, when Christ's presence will sanctify the earth and those who will be privileged to dwell on it. That will be the day in which Jerusalem will at last become the Lord's city—so appropriately renamed in Ezekiel's vision: *Yahweh Šāmâ,* "Jehovah is There" (Ezek. 48:35).

NOTES

1. Zadok was the high priest during the reign of King David. The lineage of Israel's legitimate high priests descended from his line, through which John the Baptist came into the world.

2. As we will see in greater detail in chapter 21, Joseph Smith taught that to make the Restoration complete, sacrifice will be restored, though not those sacrifices that were revealed with the law of Moses. But because animal sacrifice ended with Christ, it seems likely that the sacrifice of which the Prophet spoke will be a short-term or one-time event in fulfillment of Malachi 3:3–4, to signal that the Levites are again in the covenant and have assumed their rightful priesthood function in the house of Israel. See Andrew F. Ehat and Lyndon W. Cook, eds., *The Words of Joseph Smith: The Contemporary Accounts of the Nauvoo Discourses of the Prophet Joseph* (Provo, Utah: Religious Studies Center, Brigham Young University, 1980), 42–44.

3. Elder Bruce R. McConkie stated, "There is only one place under the whole heavens where the keys of temple building are found. There is only one people who know how to build temples and what to do in them when they are completed. That people is the Latter-day Saints." *Millennial Messiah* (Salt Lake City: Deseret Book, 1982), 279; see also 280.

4. On 6 April 1843, Joseph Smith stated, as recorded by Willard Richards: "Jerusalem must be rebuilt. Judah return, must return & the temple water come out from under the temple—the waters of the dead sea be healed.—it will take some time to build the walls & the Temple. &c & all this must be done before Son of Man will make his appe[ara]nce, wars & rumours of wars. signs in the heavens above on the earth beneath Sun turned into darkness moon to blood. earthquakes in divers places, oceans heaving beyond their bound." Based on the edited version of this passage in *Teachings of the Prophet Joseph Smith,* some argue that a temple must be

built in Jerusalem before the second coming of Jesus. It appears, however, that the passage may not have been edited well. The events in the first part of the passage (before "&c &") fit much better in a millennial context, and the list of things that "must be done before [the] Son of Man will make his appearance" most likely begins with "wars & rumours of wars." Moreover, for all we know from the original manuscript, the "&c &" may represent some omitted words and the passing of some time. Joseph Smith Diary, 6 April 1843, recorded by Willard Richards, MS 155, Box 1 folder 6, 75–76, Church Archives, The Church of Jesus Christ of Latter-day Saints, Salt Lake City, Utah, in Richard E. Turley Jr., ed., *Selected Collections from the Archives of The Church of Jesus Christ of Latter-day Saints* (Provo, Utah: Brigham Young University Press, 2002), vol. 1, DVD 20; see also Joseph Smith, *History of The Church of Jesus Christ of Latter-day Saints,* ed. B. H. Roberts, 2d ed. rev., 7 vols. (Salt Lake City: The Church of Jesus Christ of Latter-day Saints, 1932–51), 5:337; Joseph Smith, *Teachings of the Prophet Joseph Smith,* sel. Joseph Fielding Smith (Salt Lake City: Deseret Book, 1976), 286–87.

18

NEBUCHADNEZZAR'S DREAM

Daniel was a prophet who, as a young man in the days of Lehi, was taken captive to Babylonia in the Jews' exile there. The book that bears his name records some of his experiences as well as some of his dramatic, apocalyptic visions. Modern revelation explains, in specific terms, two important parts of his book—Nebuchadnezzar's dream in chapter 2 and the vision of the Ancient of Days in chapter 7 (see chapter 19 in this volume). Among Latter-day Saints, one of the most well-known Old Testament prophecies is the remarkable dream of King Nebuchadnezzar with its interpretation by Daniel. From the days of the Prophet Joseph Smith to the present, it has been understood to be a prophecy that foretells the growth and divinely established destiny of the latter-day kingdom of God on earth—The Church of Jesus Christ of Latter-day Saints.[1] Doctrine and Covenants 65 is the key modern revelation that provides a powerful commentary on Daniel 2 and makes certain its interpretation.

KINGDOMS OF GOLD, SILVER, BRONZE, IRON, AND CLAY

Nebuchadnezzar, king of Babylon, had a dream in which he saw a large statue in the shape of a man, constructed of various substances: "This image's head was of fine gold, his breast and his arms of silver, his belly and his thighs of brass, his legs of iron, his feet part of iron and part of clay" (Dan. 2:32–33). As the dream unfolded, Nebuchadnezzar saw "that a stone was cut out without hands, which smote the image upon his feet that were of iron and clay, and brake them to pieces. Then was the iron, the clay, the brass, the silver, and the gold, broken to pieces together, and became like the chaff of the summer threshingfloors; and the wind carried them away, that no place was found for them: and the stone that smote the image became a great mountain, and filled the whole earth" (Dan. 2:34–35). Daniel explained the vision. The head of gold represented Nebuchadnezzar and his kingdom. Daniel told how Nebuchadnezzar's empire would be succeeded by another, represented in the dream as the breast and arms of silver, and then by another, characterized as the bronze belly and thighs. (What we now call "brass" was first developed long after the biblical period. The King James Version word *brass* means "bronze.") That kingdom would be followed in turn by another, represented as legs of iron. The last kingdom was represented as the feet of the image, "part of iron and part of clay."

The king's dream clearly represents a historical time line—a list of successive developments in the history of the world. In Daniel's inspired interpretation, we can trace a succession of kingdoms from the days of Daniel to a later time when the kingdoms of the world would be replaced by the one kingdom established by God. As the outline of history since Daniel's day is well known, a reasonably sure interpretation of the broad meaning of the vision can be proposed. The starting point of the time line is certain—Nebuchadnezzar's Babylonian kingdom. The end point is also certain—the latter days in which we now live, in which the Church of Jesus Christ is established as the precursor for the Lord's millennial kingdom. Details in between can be suggested, but their exact interpretation is uncertain and, in fact, not even necessary.

The empire over which Nebuchadnezzar ruled is referred to technically as the Neo-Babylonian empire. Its power over Mesopotamia and surrounding areas lasted approximately from 610 B.C. to 539 B.C. Nebuchadnezzar, its chief architect, controlled almost the entirety of the Near East. His domain extended from southern Mesopotamia in the east to Upper Egypt in the southwest. As Daniel explained, this empire was the golden head of the image. It is of interest to note that each succeeding power is characterized by a metal of lesser value than the one mentioned before it. On the other hand, each succeeding metal is stronger than the previous one.[2] History shows that following Nebuchadnezzar's time, each of the succeeding empires that ruled the Near East and the Mediterranean region was more powerful than that which preceded it. But the choice of metals may simply indicate that a sequence is being represented, because the purpose of the dream was not to show relative strength or value but the passage of time and a succession of rule from one to the next.

The second world power in succession was the Persian empire, which lasted from 539 B.C. to 330 B.C. When the city of Babylon was conquered by Cyrus in 539 B.C., the Persian monarch assumed control of the vast territory that had been ruled by the Babylonians, and for most people of the Near East, the conquest was heralded as an act of liberation. The Persians extended the borders of their empire beyond the boundaries acquired by the Babylonians before them. In Daniel's visionary view, their kingdom is likely the silver breast and arms of the image in Nebuchadnezzar's dream. The next great kingdom to rule the biblical world was the empire of Alexander the Great and his successors (330–63 B.C.). Alexander set out from Greece in 334 B.C. and in a short time had control of the vast territory held by the Persians. He extended beyond it to create the largest empire that had ever existed. This may be the kingdom characterized as the belly and thighs of bronze. Alexander was not successful in creating a dynasty of his own descendants. At his death, his kingdom was divided among his generals, and it was ruled by their descendants and others until they, in turn, were overthrown by an even stronger power. The Romans conquered much of the territory of the Greeks who succeeded Alexander the Great, and they ruled the Near East from 63 B.C. to A.D. 636.[3] In the eastern Mediterranean region, the Roman empire remained until the Muslim conquest of the seventh century after Christ. Perhaps the Romans were the legs of iron in Nebuchadnezzar's dream, yet they did not rule over Babylon, the city in which the revelation came.

In Daniel's day, the entire world, as known to Daniel and his Near Eastern contemporaries, was under the control of the king of Babylon. His was truly a world empire from the point of view of their time. The realm of Persia, which followed, was similarly a kingdom that ruled the entire world, as was the empire of Alexander the Great. From a certain perspective, the same can be said of the Roman empire and the early Muslim empires in succeeding centuries. But with the fall of Rome and the later fragmentation of the Muslim empires, the world entered into an era in which one world power would no longer rule over all. Instead, for the rest of history, nations would compete for the territories once held by the great powers of the past. As with any prophetic metaphor, the imagery of the great statue is not meant to be interpreted in detail but in major concepts, and the details are often not important while the larger picture is intended to be understood. In Daniel's prophetic view of the future, the central message is clear: one world power would supersede another until there would come a time in which smaller nations would be the pattern of world government. This is the world envisioned by Daniel, a kingdom "part of iron, and part of clay, so the kingdom shall be partly strong, and partly broken" (Dan. 2:42). "And whereas thou sawest iron mixed with miry clay, . . . they shall not cleave one to another, even as iron is not mixed with clay" (Dan. 2:43).

A GREAT MOUNTAIN

It would be in the context of a world with many nations that a new kingdom would be established, a kingdom that would be different from all others. Whereas the other kingdoms described would each grow out of the ruins of kingdoms that had come before, the new kingdom that Daniel envisioned would be "cut out without hands" (Dan. 2:34), meaning that it would be of divine construction rather than human. This kingdom would subdue the nations of the world, and over the course of time it would grow from a small stone into an immense mountain that would fill the entire earth. Daniel concluded: "And in the days of these kings shall the God of heaven set up a kingdom, which shall never be destroyed: and the kingdom shall not be left to other people, but it shall break in pieces and consume all these kingdoms, and it shall stand for ever" (Dan. 2:44). President Spencer W. Kimball provided an interpretation: "The Church of Jesus Christ of Latter-day Saints was restored in 1830 after numerous revelations from the divine source; and this is the kingdom, set up by the God of heaven, that would never be destroyed nor superseded, and the stone cut out of the mountain without hands that would become a great mountain and would fill the whole earth."[4] Doctrine and Covenants 65 is scriptural substantiation of the role of the Church of Jesus Christ as God's kingdom, established in the last days of world history to prepare for the coming of him who is the rightful king of the entire earth. In Hiram, Ohio, in October 1831, the Prophet Joseph Smith uttered the following words of prayer, received by revelation: "The keys of the kingdom of God are committed unto man on the earth, and from thence shall the gospel roll forth unto the ends of the earth, as the stone which is cut out of the mountain without hands shall roll forth, until it has filled the whole earth. . . . Call upon the Lord, that his kingdom may go forth upon the earth, that the inhabitants thereof may receive it, and be prepared for the days to come, in the which the Son of Man shall come down in heaven, clothed in the brightness of his glory, to meet the kingdom of God which is set up on the earth. Wherefore, may the kingdom of God go forth, that the kingdom of heaven may come" (D&C 65:2, 5–6).

The Church of Jesus Christ of Latter-day Saints is the kingdom of God on earth. Its president holds the keys of the kingdom, by the authority of which he presides over all of God's work on earth under the direction of Jesus Christ. Among the Church's primary goals is that of establishing itself ready to receive its Master at his coming. When the time is right, the Savior will return, take personal charge of his kingdom, and reign on earth for a thousand years. At that time, in fulfillment of Daniel's prophecy, the Church will be the only kingdom standing, and it will be Christ's government on earth. President Brigham Young taught:

"The Lord God Almighty has set up a kingdom that will sway the sceptre of power and authority over all the kingdoms of the world, and will never be destroyed, it is the kingdom that Daniel saw and wrote of. It may be considered treason to say that the kingdom which that Prophet foretold is actually set up; *that* we cannot help, but we know it is so, and call upon the nations to believe our testimony. The kingdom will continue to increase, to grow, to spread and prosper more and more. Every time its enemies undertake to overthrow it, it will become more extensive and powerful; instead of its decreasing, it will continue to increase, it will spread the more, become more wonderful and conspicuous to the nations, until it fills the whole earth. If such is your wish, identify your own individual interest in it, and tie yourselves thereto by every means in your power. Let every man and every woman do this, and then be willing to make every sacrifice the Lord may require; and when they have bound up their affections, time, and talents, with all they have, to the interest of the kingdom, then have they gained the victory."[5]

NOTES

1. See Joseph Fielding Smith, *Doctrines of Salvation,* comp. Bruce R. McConkie, 3 vols. (Salt Lake City: Bookcraft, 1954–56), 1:241; Gordon B. Hinckley, Boise Idaho Temple dedicatory prayer: "Father, the little stone which thou didst cut out of the mountain without hands is rolling forth to fill the earth. Guide and strengthen the messengers of the truth" (*Church News,* 27 May 1984, 7); and Latter-day Saint sources cited in notes 4 and 5 below.

2. The division of time periods into gold, silver, bronze, and iron is not unique to Daniel's prophecy. It is found in other ancient literature as well. For example, in the mythology of the Roman poet Ovid (first century after Christ), time is divided into four ages: gold, silver, bronze, and iron; *The Metamorphoses* 1.89–414.

3. The date 63 B.C. indicates Pompey the Great's conquest of Palestine and its subjugation to the Roman state. Though much of Alexander's realm had fallen already to Roman rule, most of Syria and Mesopotamia were conquered only later. The areas east of the Tigris never were conquered by Rome. The date A.D. 636 identifies the time when Roman control ceased in the eastern Mediterranean.

4. Kimball, Conference Report, April 1976, 10.

5. Young, *Journal of Discourses,* 26 vols. (Liverpool: Latter-day Saints' Book Depot, 1854–86), 1:202–3.

19

AT ADAM-ONDI-AHMAN

Jesus' second coming will be a public event. As Joseph Smith taught, "Every eye shall see it."[1] It will be as obvious as the sun coming up in the morning, traveling across the sky, and casting light over the whole earth (see JS–M 1:26). Jesus will be seen on the land, on the oceans, and on the islands of the sea. His voice will be "heard among all people" (D&C 133:20–21). But in addition to his coming in glory to all the world, the scriptures suggest that other appearances on a smaller scale will be part of his second coming. Among those will be an appearance to a great gathering of Saints and priesthood leaders at Adam-ondi-Ahman. In May 1838, in what is now Daviess County in northwestern Missouri, Joseph Smith's clerk reported how the Prophet identified the location of that meeting: "Spring Hill" was "a name appropriated by the brethren present. But afterwards [it was] named by the mouth of [the] Lord and was called Adam-ondi-Ahman, because, said he, it is the place where Adam shall come to visit his people, or the Ancient of Days shall sit, as spoken of by Daniel the prophet."[2]

Joseph Smith understood Adam to be a man of great significance in God's plan: "Christ is the great High Priest; Adam next."[3] The Prophet taught: "The priesthood was first given to

Adam; he obtained the first presidency and held the keys of it from generation to generation. He obtained it in the creation before the world was formed. . . . He had dominion given him over every living creature. He is Michael, the archangel spoken of in the scriptures. . . . The keys [of the priesthood] have to be brought from heaven whenever the gospel is sent. When they are revealed from heaven, it is by Adam's authority. . . . The Father called all spirits before him at the creation of man and organized them. He (Adam) is the head; [he] was told to multiply. The keys were given to him and by him to others, and he will have to give an account of his stewardship, and they to him."[4] We learn in the Doctrine and Covenants that the Lord "hath appointed Michael your prince, and established his feet, and set him upon high, and given unto him the keys of salvation under the counsel and direction of the Holy One, who is without beginning of days or end of life" (D&C 78:16). Thus Adam presides under Christ over all the human family, and he holds the keys of the priesthood for them.

The latter-day gathering at Adam-ondi-Ahman will not be the first time that Adam will have convened a meeting there. In a revelation to Joseph Smith, we learn: "Three years previous to the death of Adam, he called Seth, Enos, Cainan, Mahalaleel, Jared, Enoch, and Methuselah, who were all high priests, with the residue of his posterity who were righteous, into the valley of Adam-ondi-Ahman, and there bestowed upon them his last blessing. And the Lord appeared unto them, and they rose up and blessed Adam, and called him Michael, the prince, the archangel. And the Lord administered comfort unto Adam, and said unto him: I have set thee to be at the head; a multitude of nations shall come of thee, and thou art a prince over them forever. And Adam stood up in the midst of the congregation; and, notwithstanding he was bowed down with age, being full of the Holy Ghost, predicted whatsoever should befall his posterity unto the latest generation" (D&C 107:53–56).

While in exile among the Jews in Babylonia, the prophet Daniel saw a vision of Adam's return to Adam-ondi-Ahman in the last days (see Dan. 7). He told how the kingdoms of the world would lose their dominions, to be replaced ultimately by the kingdom of God. A great gathering would convene in which Christ (the Son of Man) and Adam (the Ancient of Days) would be the major participants. Daniel wrote: "I beheld till the thrones were cast down, and the Ancient of days did sit, whose garment was white as snow, and the hair of his head like the pure wool. . . . Thousand thousands ministered unto him, and ten thousand times ten thousand stood before him. . . . I saw in the night visions, and, behold, one like the Son of man came with the clouds of heaven, and came to the Ancient of days, and they brought him near before him. And there was given him dominion, and glory, and a kingdom, that all people, nations, and languages, should serve him: his dominion is an everlasting dominion, which shall not pass away, and his kingdom that which shall not be destroyed" (Dan. 7:9–10, 13–14). Explaining this passage, the Prophet Joseph Smith said:

"Daniel speaks of the Ancient of Days; he means the oldest man, our Father Adam, Michael. He will call his children together and hold a council with them to prepare them for the coming of the Son of Man. He (Adam) is the father of the human family and presides over the spirits of all men, and all that have had the keys must stand before him in this great council. . . . The Son of Man stands before him, and there is given him glory and dominion. Adam delivers up his stewardship to Christ, that which was delivered to him as holding the keys of the universe, but retains his standing as head of the human family. . . .

"Those men to whom these keys have been given will have to be there; they without us cannot be made perfect. These men are in heaven, but their children are on earth. Their bowels yearn over us. . . . All these authoritative characters will come down and join hand in hand in bringing about this work. . . . We cannot be made perfect without them, nor they without us. When these things are done, the Son of Man will descend [and] the Ancient of Days sit."[5]

This meeting apparently will include some who will be living on earth at the time and others who will have gone already to the spirit world and to the resurrection. In it, all who have held keys will make an accounting of their stewardships to Adam, who is their presiding authority. Elder Bruce R. McConkie asked concerning those who will be in attendance, "Are they not the ones who are called to report their stewardships and to give an accounting of how and in what manner they have exercised the keys of the kingdom in their days? Will not every steward be called upon to tell what he has done with the talents with which he was endowed? Truly, it shall be so; and those who minister unto the Ancient of Days are indeed the ministers of Christ reporting their labors to their immediate superiors, even back to Adam."[6] Joseph Smith taught: "This then is the nature of the priesthood, every man holding the presidency of his dispensation and one man holding the presidency of them all, even Adam, and Adam receiving his presidency and authority from Christ. But [he] cannot receive a fulness until Christ shall present the kingdom to the Father, which shall be at the end of the last dispensation."[7]

With the keys of the ministries of all men in the hands of their patriarch, the crowning event of the great gathering will then take place. The Lord Jesus Christ will appear, and Adam, in his capacity as president and representative of all the human family, will make our collective accounting to the Lord, returning to him all the keys and powers that had been entrusted to the hands of mortal men. Thus, in the fullest sense, it will be then that "the kingdoms of this world are become the kingdoms of our Lord, and of his Christ; and he shall reign for ever and ever" (Rev. 11:15).

The time when this event will happen has not been made known in the scriptures. Joseph Smith said that Adam would call his children to the meeting "to prepare them for the coming of the Son of Man."[8] Presumably this refers to the Lord's coming in glory, not simply to his appearance at the council at Adam-ondi-Ahman. Perhaps this great gathering—in which Jesus will be acknowledged by his Saints as king and in which the keys of the kingdom held by his servants will be accounted for and returned to him from whom all authority on earth derives—will be the final event that will take place before He will appear in royal glory and majesty to all the world, at last to be acknowledged by all people as "KING OF KINGS, AND LORD OF LORDS" (Rev. 19:16).

NOTES

1. Andrew F. Ehat and Lyndon W. Cook, eds., *The Words of Joseph Smith: The Contemporary Accounts of the Nauvoo Discourses of the Prophet Joseph* (Provo, Utah: Religious Studies Center, Brigham Young University, 1980), 181; spelling, punctuation, and capitalization have been standardized in these references where necessary for readability.

2. Dean C. Jessee, ed., *Papers of Joseph Smith, Vol. 2: Journal, 1832–1842* (Salt Lake City: Deseret Book, 1992), 244–45. See Doctrine and Covenants 116.

3. Ehat and Cook, eds., *Words of Joseph Smith*, 9.

4. Ehat and Cook, eds., *Words of Joseph Smith*, 8–9.

5. Ehat and Cook, eds., *Words of Joseph Smith*, 8–10.

6. Bruce R. McConkie, *The Millennial Messiah: The Second Coming of the Son of Man* (Salt Lake City: Deseret Book, 1982), 584–85.

7. Ehat and Cook, eds., *Words of Joseph Smith*, 40.

8. Ehat and Cook, eds., *Words of Joseph Smith*, 9.

20

DREAMS, VISIONS, BLOOD, FIRE, AND PILLARS OF SMOKE

The prophecies of Joel seem to be completely removed from the context of the time and place in which they were revealed. Joel probably prophesied in Jerusalem's post-Exilic community about 500 B.C., but his book contains no explicit historical indicators to assist us in its dating. This absence of contemporary references seems to be deliberate; it is as though Joel wanted us to leave behind all thoughts of the here and now and join him in his visions of the future. Aside from the names of Joel and his father in Joel 1:1, it appears that every word in the book refers to the latter days—from the time of the Prophet Joseph Smith into the Millennium. Joel's apocalyptic style makes his fundamental message very clear: in a dramatic way, God will bring judgment upon the world, destroying evil and blessing the righteous with millennial peace and happiness.

When the angel Moroni appeared to Joseph Smith during the night of 21–22 September 1823, he taught the young Prophet about the Book of Mormon and about his role in bringing it forth (see JS–H 1:33–35). Then he taught him of his broader mission and of God's work in the latter days—from that moment into the Millennium. The angel did that by teaching him from the scriptures, carefully quoting and discussing passages from the Bible

161

that emphasized the opening of the heavens with modern revelation, spiritual gifts, and priesthood power; the gathering and
restoration of Israel; the destruction of the world and the purification of the earth; the deliverance of the faithful; the second coming of Jesus; and the blessings of the Saints in the Millennium (see
JS–H 1:36–41).[1] Among the passages that Moroni quoted was Joel
2:28–32, which begins with the following revelation (verses formatted according to Joel's Hebrew poetry):

> And it shall come to pass afterward, that I will pour
>   out my spirit upon all flesh;
> and your sons and your daughters shall prophesy,
> your old men shall dream dreams,
> your young men shall see visions:
> and also upon the servants and upon the hand-
>   maids in those days will I pour out my spirit.
>   (Joel 2:28–29)

The apostle Peter quoted and applied this same passage in the
context of the outpouring of the Spirit to the early Christians on
the day of Pentecost (see Acts 2:16–18). The phenomenon that
Peter witnessed was a remarkable parallel to what Joel foresaw, but
the actual fulfillment of the prophecy would be in the latter days.
Moroni told Joseph Smith that the revelation "was not yet
fulfilled, but was soon to be" (JS–H 1:41). If, in September 1823,
Joel's words had not yet been fulfilled but would be fulfilled soon,
then when can we look for their fulfillment? The Millennium will
be the greatest era of fulfillment, because it will be then that "the
earth shall be full of the knowledge of the Lord, as the waters
cover the sea" (Isa. 11:9). But prior to that day would come the
day of the Restoration, in which all of the spiritual gifts known
among people of earlier times would be restored again to earth.
The Lord's Saints have spiritual experiences today, and it may be
that the time of spiritual outpouring, which Moroni said "was

soon to be," has already arrived. Beginning with the First Vision and Moroni's coming, the heavens have been open in unique ways.

What are the spiritual blessings of which Joel prophesied—the pouring out of the Spirit, prophecy, dreams, and visions? Often when we think of spiritual manifestations, we think of dramatic events such as visions, healings, and speaking in tongues. But the blessings of which Joel spoke are not restricted to those. Perhaps the greatest fulfillment of Joel's words is in the quiet witness that faithful Saints receive in answer to their humble prayers concerning the truthfulness of the gospel and the divine mission of the Church. In sheer numbers and human impact, the most powerful manifestation of the Spirit today is the personal revelation that transforms lives and gives testimonies to the sons, daughters, old and young, servants and handmaids of the Church. God's Spirit is at work among the Latter-day Saints as they quietly "prophesy"—enjoy personal revelation in their lives—"dream dreams," "see visions," and otherwise enjoy the blessings of the gift of the Holy Ghost. And outside of the Church, many people have been, and continue to be, guided by the Spirit to believe in Jesus Christ and to bless the world through deeds of faith and virtue.

Moroni also quoted the rest of Joel, chapter 2:

> And I will shew wonders in the heavens and in the
>   earth,
> blood, and fire, and pillars of smoke.
> The sun shall be turned into darkness,
> and the moon into blood,
> before the great and the terrible day of the Lord
>   come. (Joel 2:30–31)

This prophecy is found in all of the standard works of the Church, testifying that it is real, that it is important, and that we will witness dramatic things as the earth is being cleansed for the coming of Christ (see Matt. 24:29; 1 Ne. 22:18–19; D&C 45:40–42; JS–M 1:33).[2] Whatever these calamities are, and however they eventually will come to pass, it seems safe to say that they have not happened yet to the fullest degree. We would know it if they had. But for the righteous, this will not be a day of calamity, though it will be both "great" and "terrible."[3] As Joel reminded us, those who "call on the name of the Lord shall be delivered" and will find safety among the Lord's Saints in Zion (Joel 2:32). And as Nephi taught, "Wherefore, he will preserve the righteous by his power. . . . Wherefore, the righteous need not fear; for thus saith the prophet, they shall be saved" (1 Ne. 22:17).

NOTES

1. See Kent P. Jackson, *From Apostasy to Restoration* (Salt Lake City: Deseret Book, 1996), 102–15.

2. See also Acts 2:19–21; Doctrine and Covenants 29:14; 88:88–91.

3. See Dana M. Pike, "The Great and Dreadful Day of the Lord: The Anatomy of an Expression," *BYU Studies* 41, no. 2 (2002): 149–60.

21

JESUS, MORONI, AND MALACHI

Malachi was a prophet who preached to the Jews in Jerusalem not long after their return from their Babylonian exile, probably around 500 B.C. or a few years later.[1] For Latter-day Saints, Malachi's words are among the most well-known in the Old Testament. Although the first half of his book deals with conditions of his own time, chapters 3 and 4 are particularly relevant to the days in which we now live. As Jesus met with the children of Lehi after his resurrection, he quoted from those later chapters (see 3 Ne. 24–25). Their latter-day focus is probably why the Lord directed that they be written in the Nephite record and probably also why Mormon was inspired to include them for us in his Book of Mormon abridgment. Centuries later, on the night of 21–22 September 1823, Mormon's son, the angel Moroni, appeared to Joseph Smith and taught him about God's latter-day work on the earth. Among the passages of scripture that he quoted were parts of chapters 3 and 4 of Malachi (see JS–H 1:36–39).[2] If those chapters were important enough that Jesus quoted them to the Nephites and Lamanites and Moroni quoted them to Joseph Smith, then certainly they have a message that we need to know.

Malachi, "My Messenger," is a very odd form for an ancient Hebrew name. Indeed, it is probably not a real name at all but a

pen name drawn by the author, or by a later editor, from words in
Malachi 3:1. Because of the fragmented nature of some of the
material in chapters 3 and 4, in which diverse topics are discussed, these chapters have the feel not of a continuous prophecy
but of a collection of utterances—a Malachi quote book.

MALACHI 3

Joseph Smith stated that Moroni "quoted part of the third
chapter of Malachi" (JS–H 1:36), although he did not mention
which of its eighteen verses were quoted. In the Book of Mormon,
Jesus quoted the chapter in its entirety (see 3 Ne. 24). Malachi 3
is rich in powerful passages that have a direct bearing on the
Dispensation of the Fulness of Times that was being introduced,
in part, by Moroni's visit to Joseph Smith. The revelation in the
first two verses foretells the appearance of the Lord's messenger
who would be sent to prepare the way before him. It tells of the
coming of the Lord "suddenly" to his temple and asks, "Who may
abide the day of his coming? and who shall stand when he
appeareth?" The context is the Second Coming, yet Malachi's
prophecy is used in the New Testament to describe the mission of
John the Baptist, the messenger sent to prepare the way before
Christ's coming in mortality (see Matt. 11:10; Mark 1:2). The passage is rightly applied to John, but the ultimate fulfillment will be
in the latter days. Many messengers have been involved in preparing the way for Christ, participating in the restoration of the
gospel, and laying the groundwork for the Millennium. Some of
those messengers have been mortal and some angelic. Among the
heavenly messengers of the Restoration, the following could be
listed: John the Baptist and Peter, James, and John, who restored
priesthood power to Joseph Smith; Elijah, the bearer of priesthood
keys whose coming is the subject of discussion in Malachi 4:5–6;
and Moroni, the heavenly messenger who brought forth the Book

of Mormon and assisted Joseph Smith in his calling. Perhaps what Malachi envisioned was not an individual but the collective ministry of all the heavenly messengers who restored doctrine and keys in the last days, each in turn preparing the way for Christ.

The Prophet Joseph Smith was also a great messenger sent to prepare the way before the Lord. As John was sent anciently, Joseph Smith was sent into the world in modern times to establish the Lord's work prior to his second coming. But perhaps an even broader interpretation may be of value, which would include the entire work and mission in which Joseph Smith was engaged. The Lord revealed: "I have sent mine everlasting covenant into the world, to be a light to the world, and to be a standard for my people, and for the Gentiles to seek to it, and to be a messenger before my face to prepare the way before me" (D&C 45:9). Thus the gospel—restored in the latter days to make the world ready for the Lord—is a messenger sent before him.

As Malachi foretold, when Christ comes he will "purify the sons of Levi," "that they may offer unto the Lord an offering in righteousness" (Mal. 3:3). The descendants of Levi are the rightful heirs to the Aaronic Priesthood under the law of Moses. Thousands of them still exist among the Jews throughout the world today and have preserved their identity through family names and traditions. They do not now enjoy either the priesthood or the gospel covenants, which are found in the Lord's Church, and thus for the present they are unable to fill the role to which their family was called by revelation and set apart in ancient times. As an aspect of the restoration of all things, the tribe of Levi will once again fill a priesthood function in the Lord's kingdom, but it can only come after they have become converted and "purified," and after they have joined the Church of Jesus Christ and have been restored to their place under the direction of its leaders. Joseph Smith taught:

"All the ordinances and duties that ever have been required by the priesthood under the direction and commandments of the Almighty, in any of the dispensations, shall all be had in the last dispensation. Therefore all things had under the authority of the priesthood at any former period shall be had again—bringing to pass the restoration spoken of by the mouth of all the holy prophets. Then shall the sons of Levi offer an acceptable sacrifice to the Lord.

"... It is generally supposed that sacrifice was entirely done away when the great sacrifice was offered up and that there will be no necessity for the ordinance of sacrifice in [the] future. But those who assert this are certainly not acquainted with the duties, privileges, and authority of the priesthood, or with the prophets. ... We frequently have mention made of the offering of sacrifice by the servants of the Most High in ancient days prior to the law of Moses, which ordinances will be continued when the priesthood is restored with all its authority, power, and blessings. ... These sacrifices as well as every ordinance belonging to the priesthood will, when the temple of the Lord shall be built and the sons [of] Levi be purified, be fully restored and attended to—then all their powers, ramifications, and blessings. This ever was and will exist when the powers of the Melchizedek Priesthood are sufficiently manifest. Else how can the restitution of all things spoken of by all the holy prophets be brought to pass? It is not to be understood that the law of Moses will be established again with all its rites and variety of ceremonies; this had never been spoken of by the prophets. But those things which existed prior [to] Moses' day, namely sacrifice, will be continued."[3]

From this passage we learn that the descendants of Levi will offer animal sacrifice in the Millennium, in restoration of those offerings which were in force prior to the law of Moses. From what the Prophet taught, it is uncertain whether this will be a lasting, ongoing, ordinance or a short-term event to complete the cycle of the restoration of all things and signal that the Levites are again in the covenant and have assumed their rightful priesthood function in the house of Israel.[4] In any case, it will be done under the Lord's direction and by means of the keys of the priesthood that are in his Church. Those keys were restored to the world when John the Baptist, the last holder of the keys in ancient times, conferred them on Joseph Smith. When he did so, he stated, "This shall never be taken again from the earth, until the sons of Levi do offer again an offering unto the Lord in righteousness" (D&C 13:1; JS–H 1:69). Oliver Cowdery recalled that John said that the restored Aaronic Priesthood would "remain upon earth, *that* the sons of Levi may yet offer an offering unto the Lord in righteousness."[5] The Doctrine and Covenants uses the term "sons of Moses and of Aaron" for those who receive and magnify their priesthood (see D&C 84:31–34). They will "offer an acceptable offering and sacrifice in the house of the Lord" (D&C 84:31). In another revelation, the Lord includes "your memorials for your sacrifices by the sons of Levi" among those things that "are ordained by the ordinance" of the temple (D&C 124:39). These Doctrine and Covenants references suggest figurative fulfillments of Malachi 3:3, in addition to the sacrifice of which Joseph Smith spoke. As the Prophet taught, "The Lord will purify the sons of Levi, good or bad, for it is through them that blessings flow to Israel. . . . And then, and not till then, 'shall the offering of Judah and Jerusalem be pleasant unto the Lord, as in days of old and as in former years' [Mal. 3:4]."[6]

One matter of concern specified by the Lord through Malachi is tithing. Jesus quoted Malachi's words regarding it to the children of Lehi (see 3 Ne. 24:8–12), and he restored the principle to the Church in the latter days (see D&C 119:4). Latter-day Saints who have put the Lord to the test, as he invited (see Mal. 3:10), can testify to the fulfillment of God's promises. It is not unlikely that the law of tithing was an important part of the Lord's plan for his Saints in all dispensations, as it is for us today (see Gen.

14:18–20; 28:20–22). Malachi's revelations drew a stark contrast between those who are humble and receptive to the Lord's will and those who are not. Those who revere the Lord can rejoice that their righteousness is recorded in God's "book of remembrance" (Mal. 3:16). Their reward is sure: "They shall be mine, saith the Lord of Hosts, in that day when I make up my jewels" (Mal. 3:17). The relevance of this section of Malachi to Jesus' audience in early America seems clear: Those who did not trust the prophetic announcements of his coming—and thus did not prepare—were cut off. Yet those who were faithful enjoyed the Savior's presence, even then (see 3 Ne. 27:30–31).

MALACHI 4

Jesus quoted Malachi 4 in its entirety to the children of Lehi (see 3 Ne. 25), and Moroni quoted it as well to Joseph Smith (see JS–H 1:36). The setting for the fulfillment of this chapter is the destruction of the wicked that will be part of the earth's cleansing preparatory to the Lord's return in glory. Whether by repentance or by destruction, wickedness in all forms must be removed before Christ will dwell here, for only those who are worthy will be privileged to live in his presence, and "all that do wickedly, shall be stubble" (Mal. 4:1).

In the Joseph Smith–History, the Prophet did not quote or mention specifically Malachi 4:2–4, although Moroni quoted the entire chapter to him. Verses 2 and 3 continue the theme of the cleansing that will attend the Second Coming. The Lord foretold the condition of those who "fear [his] name." For them, "the Sun of Righteousness [will] arise with healing in his wings." In the Bible, the word *Sun* is used, whereas the Book of Mormon uses *Son*. The translators of the King James Version correctly recognized the term "Sun of righteousness" as an allusion to the Lord, noting this by the use of the capital letter in the word *Sun*. Their interpretation is borne out by the Book of Mormon, where the phrase is personified completely—"Son of Righteousness" (3 Ne. 25:2). Verse 3 speaks of the righteous treading on the wicked in that day of the Lord's justice, which should be interpreted in the context of the overall destruction of evil and the ultimate victory of good over bad. The setting in which Jesus quoted this passage in the Book of Mormon helps us understand its relevance to the situation of his listeners. The Savior's visit to the Americas provides a pattern that will be followed on a worldwide scale before, and at the time of, his second coming.[7] As Malachi foretold, the day of the Lord's coming is one of destruction for the wicked, while for the righteous it will be a day of unimaginable blessings (see Mal. 4:1–2). What could better describe what the faithful Nephites and Lamanites had gone through and were then experiencing? The "Son of Righteousness" had arisen in their midst, "with healing in his wings" (3 Ne. 25:2).

Malachi 4:4 states: "Remember ye the law of Moses my servant, which I commanded unto him in Horeb for all Israel," seemingly a reminder to observe the law of Moses—in force in Malachi's day but fulfilled in Christ. Much of the book of Malachi has to do with the law and the priests who administered it. But perhaps Malachi's statement hints at something else. Joseph Smith, in commenting on this verse, taught: "[The] law revealed to Moses in Horeb never was revealed to the children of Israel,"[8] apparently referring to the higher law revealed to Moses which Israel did not receive because of rebellion (see JST Ex. 34:1–2; D&C 84:23–25). It may be that the intent of Jesus and Moroni in quoting the verse was to draw attention to that higher law. Jesus' listeners in early America were worthy and able to have the higher law, the Melchizedek Priesthood, and the ordinances and blessings that God revealed to Moses on the mountain but which their Israelite ancestors had forfeited.

THE COMING OF ELIJAH

When Moroni appeared to Joseph Smith in September 1823, he quoted Malachi 4:5–6 differently from how it is recorded either in the Bible or in the Book of Mormon: "Behold, I will reveal unto you the Priesthood, by the hand of Elijah the prophet, before the coming of the great and dreadful day of the Lord. And he shall plant in the hearts of the children the promises made to the fathers, and the hearts of the children shall turn to their fathers. If it were not so, the whole earth would be utterly wasted at his coming" (JS–H 1:38–39; see also D&C 2). This passage, in either version, is one of the most important scriptures of the Restoration, because it foretells the creation of links of priesthood power that bind and seal both ordinances and generations on earth and in heaven. The prophecy of Elijah's coming was fulfilled on 3 April 1836, as the ancient prophet who held the keys of sealing power appeared in the Kirtland Temple to the founding prophet of the last dispensation to restore those keys to the earth (see D&C 110:13–16).

In the recorded teachings and writings of Joseph Smith, the Prophet taught on the subject of Malachi 4:5–6 more than on any other passage of scripture.[9] Among other things, he taught: "Elijah was the last prophet that held the keys of this priesthood, and who will, before the last dispensation, restore the authority and deliver the keys of this priesthood in order that all the ordinances may be attended to in righteousness. . . . Why send Elijah? Because he holds the keys of the authority to administer in all the ordinances of the priesthood, and without the authority the ordinances could not be administered in righteousness."[10] The priesthood keys restored by Elijah provide the sealing power for all ordinances of the priesthood, making those performed on earth valid in the heavens and enabling worthy couples and families to be sealed together for the eternities. On another occasion, the

Prophet taught: "Now the word 'turn' here should be translated 'bind' or 'seal.' But what is the object of this important mission, or how is it to be fulfilled? The keys are to be delivered, the spirit of Elijah is to come, the gospel to be established, the Saints of God gathered, Zion built up, and the Saints to come up as saviors on Mount Zion. But how are they to become saviors on Mount Zion? By building their temples, erecting their baptismal fonts, and going forth and receiving all the ordinances, baptisms, confirmations, washings, anointings, ordinations, and sealing powers upon our heads in behalf of all our progenitors who are dead, and redeem them that they may come forth in the first resurrection and be exalted to thrones of glory with us. And herein is the chain that binds the hearts of the fathers to the children, and the children to the fathers, which fulfills the mission of Elijah."[11] Ordinances performed on earth are valid in the eternities, and ordinances can be performed by this power on earth in behalf of those who are already in the spirit world. Thus Elijah's coming makes temple work for the dead possible and provides the welding link between generations.

Perhaps the Savior's visit to the Nephites initiated an era of intense temple activity among them, and perhaps Malachi's prophecy was used to stress eternal marriage and the other blessings of Elijah's sealing power (see 4 Ne. 1:11). Moroni's quoting of this passage to Joseph Smith was part of the young Prophet's training for his life's mission, and the subsequent restoration of keys and doctrines enables us to enjoy the blessings of the sealing power in our temples and homes today.

NOTES

1. See Andrew E. Hill, *Malachi*, Anchor Bible 25D (New York: Doubleday, 1998), 77–84.

2. See Kent P. Jackson, *From Apostasy to Restoration* (Salt Lake City: Deseret Book, 1996), 102–15.

3. Andrew F. Ehat and Lyndon W. Cook, eds., *The Words of Joseph Smith: The Contemporary Accounts of the Nauvoo Discourses of the Prophet Joseph* (Provo, Utah: Religious Studies Center, Brigham Young University, 1980), 42–44; see also 50–51, n. 1; spelling, punctuation, and capitalization have been standardized where necessary for readability.

4. See Joseph Fielding Smith, *Doctrines of Salvation,* comp. Bruce R. McConkie, 3 vols. (Salt Lake City: Bookcraft, 1954–56), 3:93–94 ("long enough to complete the fulness of the restoration"); and Bruce R. McConkie, *Mormon Doctrine,* 2d ed. (Salt Lake City: Bookcraft, 1966), 666 ("apparently on a one-time basis"). Given that there will be no death in the Millennium, these interpretations seem appropriate.

5. *Latter Day Saints' Messenger and Advocate* 1, no. 1 (October 1834): 16; emphasis added; note at JS–H 1:71.

6. Ehat and Cook, eds., *Words of Joseph Smith,* 66; for President John Taylor's understanding of the Prophet's words, see *Mediation and Atonement* (Salt Lake City: Deseret News, 1882), 119–23.

7. See Ezra Taft Benson, *A Witness and a Warning: A Modern-day Prophet Testifies of the Book of Mormon* (Salt Lake City: Deseret Book, 1988), 37.

8. Ehat and Cook, eds., *Words of Joseph Smith,* 244.

9. See Joseph Smith, *Joseph Smith's Commentary on the Bible,* comp. and ed. Kent P. Jackson (Salt Lake City: Deseret Book, 1994), 69–74.

10. Ehat and Cook, eds., *Words of Joseph Smith,* 43.

11. Ehat and Cook, eds., *Words of Joseph Smith,* 318.

CONCLUSION

Joseph Smith wrote: "The dispensation of the fulness of times will bring to light the things that have been revealed in all former dispensations."[1] The phrase "bring to light" is a profound understatement for what the Restoration contributes to our knowledge of earlier times. It was, in fact, an *explosion* of light about the scriptural past, and it was a process that teaches us, if we allow it to, more about what was "revealed in all former dispensations" than most of us realize. The restored gospel touches upon every previous dispensation of history as it reveals vital knowledge concerning each one. Even more remarkably, it shines a bright light on virtually every important scriptural person who ever lived prior to our day. Consider the following list of people from the Old Testament who are illuminated in some way through the revelations and teachings of Joseph Smith—in some cases dramatically:[2] Adam (D&C 27:11; Moses 1:34), Eve (1 Ne. 5:11; D&C 138:39), Cain (Hel. 6:27; Moses 5:18), Abel (D&C 84:16; Moses 5:20), Seth (D&C 107:42; Moses 6:2), Enoch (Moses 5:42), Methuselah (D&C 107:50; Moses 6:25), Noah (Alma 10:22; D&C 84:14–15), Ham (Moses 8:12, 27), Shem (D&C 138:41; Moses 8:12, 27), Japheth (Moses 8:12, 27), Melchizedek (Alma 13:14; D&C 84:14), Abraham (2 Ne. 8:2; Abr. 1:2), Sarah

175

(2 Ne. 8:2; D&C 132:65), Hagar (D&C 132:34), Isaac (1 Ne. 6:4; D&C 98:32), Jacob (3 Ne. 10:17; D&C 27:10), Levi (3 Ne. 24:3; D&C 13), Joseph (1 Ne. 5:14; D&C 27:10), Manasseh (2 Ne. 19:21), Ephraim (D&C 27:5), Jethro (D&C 84:7), Moses (1 Ne. 4:2; D&C 8:3; Moses 1:1), Aaron (D&C 84:18), Joshua (1 Ne. 17:32–35), Samuel (3 Ne. 20:24), Saul (JST 1 Sam. 28:9–15), David (2 Ne. 19:7; Jacob 1:15), Solomon (2 Ne. 5:16; D&C 132:1), Nathan (D&C 132:39), Elijah (3 Ne. 25:5; D&C 2:1), Amos,[3] Isaiah (2 Ne. 6:4; D&C 113), Jeremiah (Hel. 8:20), Ezekiel (D&C 29:21), Zedekiah (1 Ne. 1:4), Daniel (D&C 116:1), Joel (JS–H 1:41), Malachi (3 Ne. 24; D&C 110:14), and all the prophets (Jacob 7:11).

Some Old Testament people are noted only briefly in modern revelation, but even that substantiates the reality of their existence and proves "that the holy scriptures are true" (D&C 20:11). For the most important of them—Adam, Eve, Abraham, Moses, and others—the restored gospel provides new, expansive, and vital information without which their lives, teachings, and ministries cannot be understood fully. For this reason and for many others, the Restoration's contributions to the Bible are indispensable, and no Latter-day Saint should undertake to study it without making full use of modern scripture and the teachings of Joseph Smith. As the Prophet said, the Restoration is indeed a work of "vast magnitude and almost beyond the comprehension of mortals," a work "worthy of arch-angels; a work which will cast into the shade the things which have heretofore been accomplished."[4] The people whose names and lives are recorded in the Bible "have looked forward with joyful anticipation to the day in which we live, and fired with heavenly and joyful anticipations, they have sung, and written, and prophesied of this our day."[5] Perhaps the rejoicing of biblical Saints also included the satisfaction that because of the ministry of Joseph Smith, we would know them better than we could by reading the Bible alone. Indeed, through the Restoration, we understand better their lives, their revelations, the dreams and visions that motivated them, and—most important of all—their witness of our Savior Jesus Christ.

NOTES

1. *Times and Seasons* 2, no. 24 (15 October 1841): 578.

2. The references provided are far from comprehensive but are simply representative examples.

3. *Times and Seasons* 3, no. 21 (1 September 1842): 905; Andrew F. Ehat and Lyndon W. Cook, eds., *The Words of Joseph Smith: The Contemporary Accounts of the Nauvoo Discourses of the Prophet Joseph* (Provo, Utah: Religious Studies Center, Brigham Young University, 1980), 181.

4. *Times and Seasons* 1, no. 12 (October 1840): 178–79.

5. *Times and Seasons* 3, no. 13 (2 May 1842): 776; grammar and punctuation standardized.

Scripture Index

OLD TESTAMENT

Genesis
8:20, p. 21
13:14–15, 17, p. 41
14:25–50 (JST), p. 5
14:40 (JST), p. 41
15:12 (JST), p. 33
15:18, p. 41
17:8, p. 41
22:1–18, p. 21
37:5–11, p. 98
48:8–11 (JST), p. 98
48:10–22, p. 50
49:8–10, pp. 50, 98
49:22–26, p. 50
50:27–28 (JST), p. 94
50:30, p. 115
50:31, p. 115

Exodus
32:1–35, p. 13
34:1 (JST), pp. 8, 17, 30
34:1–2 (JST), pp. 9, 171

Leviticus
7:12–13, 15, 16, p. 22
11:44, p. 20
17:11, p. 26
22:18, 21, 23, 29, p. 22
26:33, p. 63

Numbers
11:1–34, p. 13
14:1–45, p. 13

Deuteronomy
4:25–27, p. 42
4:27, p. 63
10:2 (JST), p. 8
11:26–28, p. 41
14:28–29, p. 81
24:19–21, p. 81
28:64, p. 63
33:16–17, p. 98

Judges
5:19, p. 127

1 Kings
12, p. 117

2 Kings
15–17, p. 42
15:29, p. 63
17, p. 80
17:1–24, p. 117
17:3–6, p. 63
17:6, pp. 43, 51
17:7–23, p. 7
17:23, p. 63
18:13–20:19, p. 77
21:9, p. 7

2 Chronicles

35:22, p. 127

Psalms

14:2–3 (JST), p. 7
14:4 (JST), p. 18

Isaiah

1–35, pp. 72, 73
1–39, pp. 72, 75
1:10, p. 7
1:10–15, p. 37
1:15, p. 6
2–8, p. 83
2–14, p. 76
2:3–4, p. 85
2:4, 10–21, p. 89
2:5 (JST), p. 6
2:22, p. 80
3:1–8, 10–26, p. 89
3:13–15, p. 81
4:1–6, p. 89
5, p. 86
5:1, p. 86
5:1–7, p. 49
5:5–6, p. 89
5:7, p. 86
5:23, p. 81
5:25–30, p. 89
7, p. 80
7:1–8:10, p. 89
7:1–16, p. 80
7:2, p. 120
7:2–17, p. 70
7:5, 8, 9, 17, p. 120
9:6–7, p. 110
10:1–4, p. 81
10:5–19, p. 89
10:22, p. 86
10:24–34, pp. 80, 89
11, pp. 91, 94
11:1, p. 92
11:2, p. 94
11:6, pp. 91, 95
11:9, pp. 91, 95, 162
11:10, pp. 92, 93
11:10–13, p. 49

11:13, pp. 70, 120
11:16, pp. 49, 69
13:1–5, 14–22, p. 89
13:19, p. 86
17:3, p. 120
19:23, p. 49
24–27, p. 124
26:19, p. 31
28–29, p. 76
34–35, p. 77
35:8, p. 49
35:8–10, p. 69
36–37, p. 80
36–39, pp. 72, 77
39, p. 74
40, pp. 75, 76
40–55, p. 72
40–66, pp. 73, 74, 75
43:5–6, p. 69
44:1, p. 97
48–55, p. 76
49, pp. 96, 97
49:1–4, p. 98
49:1–6, p. 96
49:2, pp. 98, 99
49:3, 4, p. 99
49:5, p. 100
49:5–6, p. 99
49:6, pp. 100, 101, 102
49:16–18, 21, p. 104
49:22, p. 49
49:22–23, p. 44
53, pp. 11, 34, 82
55, p. 76
56–66, pp. 72, 77
56:6–8, p. 54
57:7–8, p. 49
59:3, 7, p. 6

Jeremiah

2:8, p. 18
2:21, p. 49
3:6–20, p. 49
5:31, p. 18
6:6–7, p. 13
6:20, p. 37
7:15, p. 120

16:13–21, p. 46
16:14–15, p. 100
16:15, p. 69
16:16–17, p. 44
16:19–21, p. 54
23:1, p. 107
23:3–4, pp. 47, 49
23:5–6, pp. 47, 110
23:7–8, p. 52
24:1–10, p. 49
30:9, p. 109
31:6, pp. 48, 100, 120
31:6–7, p. 52
31:9, p. 48
31:10, pp. 49, 107
31:31, 33–34, p. 47
32:37, p. 42
33:14–22, p. 109
33:16, p. 110
50:6, 17, p. 107

Ezekiel

2:3–7, p. 112
2:9–3:4, p. 120
3:7, p. 112
4:1–8, 9–17, p. 120
5:1–5, 12, p. 120
9:3, p. 142
10:18–19, pp. 142, 146
11:19–20, p. 49
11:22–23, pp. 142, 146
16:1–63, p. 49
20:5–8, 10–12, p. 7
20:23, p. 64
20:25, p. 7
22:2–4, 8–13, p. 13
22:26–28, p. 107
23:1–49, p. 49
33:21, p. 77
34, p. 111
34:1–31, p. 107
34:2–24, p. 49
34:11–14, p. 108
34:23, pp. 109, 110
36:26–27, p. 49
37, p. 114
37:1–14, p. 49

37:16, pp. 113, 120
37:17, p. 113
37:19, pp. 114, 120
37:21, p. 117
37:21–22, p. 114
37:22, pp. 114, 117
37:22–23, p. 116
37:23–24, p. 114
37:23–27, p. 48
37:24, p. 109
37:24–25, pp. 114, 118
37:25, pp. 109, 114, 117
37:26, p. 119
37:26–27, p. 116
38–39, pp. 124, 129, 135, 139
38:2, p. 135
38:8, pp. 135, 136
38:19–39:8, p. 135
39:9–16, 17–20, p. 136
39:25–29, p. 138
40:2, p. 141
40:5–42:20, p. 142
43:1–5, pp. 142, 146
43:13–27, pp. 143, 144
43:18–27, p. 144
44:4, pp. 142, 146
44:10–31, p. 144
44:15–16, 23, p. 143
45:13–46:23, p. 143
47:1–5, 6–10, 12, p. 143
47:13–48:29, p. 143
47:21–23, p. 144
48:35, p. 147

Daniel

2, p. 149
2:32–33, 34–35, p. 150
2:34, p. 153
2:42, p. 152
2:44, p. 153
7, pp. 149, 158
7:9–10, 13–14, p. 158
12:2, p. 31

Hosea

1:2–11, p. 49
2:1–3:3, p. 49

3:5, p. 109
4:17, p. 120
5:3, 11–14, p. 120
6:4, 10, p. 120
8:9, 11, p. 120
8:12–13, p. 37
9:3, p. 120
9:17, p. 63

Joel

1:1, p. 161
1:1–2:11, p. 129
2, p. 163
2:28–29, p. 162
2:30–31, p. 163
2:32, p. 164
3, p. 124
3:1–16, pp. 128, 129
3:2, 14, p. 128

Amos

2:4, 6–8, p. 13
5:21–23, p. 37
9:9, p. 63

Obadiah

1:18, p. 120

Micah

3:11, pp. 18, 107
6:10–13, 16, p. 13

Habakkuk

1:2–4, p. 13

Zephaniah

1:4–6, p. 13
2:1–4, p. 13
3:3–4, p. 107
3:15, p. 110

Zechariah

2:6, p. 69
9:10, 13, p. 120
10:6, p. 120
12:10, p. 130
13:2–6, p. 134
13:7–9, p. 129
14:3, p. 129
14:9, p. 110

14:12–15, p. 133

Malachi

3, p. 166
3–4, pp. 165, 166
3:1, p. 166
3:3, pp. 167, 169
3:3–4, p. 147
3:4, 10, p. 169
3:16, 17, p. 170
4, p. 170
4:1, 2–4, p. 170
4:4, p. 171
4:5–6, pp. 166, 172

NEW TESTAMENT

Matthew

1:21–55, p. 132
1:23, pp. 132, 133
1:26, p. 156
1:28, p. 133
1:28–29, p. 132
1:30, p. 137
1:31, p. 101
1:33, p. 164
3:7–10, p. 18
3:8, p. 55
3:9–10, p. 49
3:11 (JST), p. 10
5:13, 14, p. 97
5:17, p. 24
5:21, 27, p. 19
7:10, p. 11
11:10, p. 166
14:3–10, p. 18
14:5, p. 18
15:4, p. 19
15:24, p. 65
16:19, p. 93
19:18–19, p. 28
21:23, p. 18
23:30–35, p. 18
24, p. 132
24:29, p. 164
25:1–13, p. 49

Mark

1:2, p. 166
7:10, p. 28
10:19, p. 28

Luke

3:3, p. 10
3:8, 9, p. 55
3:16, p. 10
14:16–24, pp. 44, 55
14:24, p. 55
18:20, p. 28

John

1:29, p. 39
3:16, p. 24
8:56, p. 33
10:11, p. 108
10:14, pp. 97, 108, 110
10:30–31, p. 108
15:5, p. 94
21:16, p. 97

Acts

2:16–18, p. 162
2:19–21, p. 164
4:1–21, p. 28
7:51–53, p. 30
22:30–23:10, p. 28

Romans

6:3–11, p. 9
6:23, p. 26
7:7, p. 28
9:6–7, p. 55
13:9, p. 28

Galatians

3:19, pp. 5, 26, 39
3:24, p. 26
3:24 (JST), p. 14
3:24–25, p. 26
3:24–25 (JST), p. 39
3:27–29, p. 54

Ephesians

6:2–3, p. 28

Colossians

2:17, p. 11

Hebrews

4:15, p. 23
8:6, p. 15
10:18, p. 144
13:2, p. 68
13:20, p. 110

James

1:1, p. 71
2:11, p. 28

1 Peter

5:4, p. 110

Revelation

11:1–12, p. 133
11:8, p. 133
11:15, p. 159
16, pp. 126, 127
16:14, p. 127
16:16, pp. 125, 126, 127, 133
16:17–21, p. 127
17:5, p. 133
19:6–9, p. 49
19:10, p. 89
19:16, pp. 110, 160
20:8, p. 133

BOOK OF MORMON

1 Nephi

1:4, p. 176
4:2, p. 176
5:11, p. 175
5:14, p. 176
6:4, p. 176
8–14, pp. 121, 123
10:12, p. 49
10:14, p. 101
13:24–25, 26–28, p. 32
13:28, p. 32
13:39–40, p. 115
13:41, pp. 110, 115
14, p. 137
14:11–14, p. 137
14:11–17, p. 137
14:13, 14, p. 137

17:22, p. 37
17:32–35, p. 176
17:35, p. 60
19:6, p. 78
19:10, 13, 14, p. 35
19:15–16, p. 57
19:16, p. 57
19:23, pp. 75, 78
19:23–24, p. 79
19:24, p. 103
22:3, pp. 64, 87, 104
22:4, pp. 62, 64
22:7, p. 64
22:7–11, pp. 64, 68
22:8–11, p. 101
22:9, 11, 12, p. 105
22:17, 18–19, p. 164
22:24, 25, p. 110

2 Nephi

3:4–24, p. 115
3:7, p. 94
3:11, 12, p. 115
5:16, p. 176
6:4, p. 176
6:5, p. 78
6:11, p. 56
8:2, pp. 175, 176
10:7–8, p. 60
10:20–22, p. 42
11, p. 82
11:2, p. 78
11:4, p. 25
12–18, p. 83
19:7, p. 176
21:12–13, p. 70
25:1, 2, p. 88
25:4, pp. 88, 89
25:5, p. 88
25:5–6, p. 83
25:7, p. 88
25:25–27, p. 36
26:33, p. 56
29:11, p. 66
29:11–14, p. 70
29:12–13, p. 70
29:12–14, p. 67

30:2, p. 54

Jacob

1:6, p. 36
1:15, p. 176
4:5, p. 21
4:14, pp. 7, 18, 37
5, pp. 40, 49
7:11, p. 176

Mosiah

3:15, p. 11
13:29–30, p. 25
13:29–32, p. 19
13:30, pp. 20, 37
13:31, p. 25
13:32, p. 21
13:33–35, p. 34
18, p. 31
23–24, p. 31

Alma

10:3, p. 43
12:9, p. 10
13:14, p. 175
29:8, p. 14
33:11, 16, p. 35
34:8–9, p. 23
34:9, p. 23
34:10, p. 24
34:13–14, pp. 25, 144
34:16–17, p. 24
42:14, p. 23
42:15, pp. 23, 26
63:4–9, p. 71
63:8, p. 71

Helaman

3:10–12, p. 71
6:27, p. 175
8:19–20, p. 35
8:20, p. 176
15:13, p. 110

3 Nephi

1–8, p. 131
8:3, 19, p. 131
10:14–16, p. 35
10:17, p. 176

15:5, pp. 24, 29
15:17, 21, p. 110
15:23, p. 65
16:1, p. 66
16:1–3, p. 65
16:3, p. 110
16:4–5, p. 70
16:13, p. 54
17:4, pp. 62, 65, 66
20:13, pp. 64, 69
20:24, p. 176
20:30–31, p. 44
20:30–33, pp. 46, 57
20:33, p. 44
21:1, 2, p. 116
21:1–7, p. 53
21:25–29, p. 70
23:4, p. 66
24, pp. 166, 176
24–25, p. 165
24:3, p. 176
24:8–12, p. 169
25, p. 170
25:2, p. 171
25:5, p. 176
26:9–11, p. 10
27:30–31, p. 170
28:6, 27–28, p. 67
29:1, p. 116

4 Nephi
1:11, p. 173

Mormon
4:5, p. 132

Ether
13:9, p. 58
13:10–11, p. 119
13:11, pp. 58, 146

DOCTRINE AND COVENANTS

1:35, p. 132
2, p. 172
3:19–20, p. 53
8:3, p. 176
13, p. 176
19:16–17, p. 26

20:11, pp. 115, 176
27:5, pp. 114, 176
27:10, p. 115, 176
27:11, p. 175
28:8, p. 53
29:14, p. 164
29:20, p. 136
29:20–21, p. 139
29:21, pp. 140, 176
32:1–5, p. 53
35:20, p. 12
36:2, p. 27
39:11, p. 47
42:58, p. 101
45:9, p. 167
45:26, 28–29, 33, 34–36, p. 132
45:39, p. 131
45:40–50, p. 133
45:43–44, p. 59
45:46, p. 133
45:48, p. 59
45:51–53, pp. 59, 133
45:59, pp. 110, 146
45:69–70, p. 132
50:44, pp. 108, 110
63:33, p. 132
65:2, 5–6, p. 154
66:2, p. 47
77:14, p. 68
77:15–16, p. 133
78:16, p. 157
84:7, p. 176
84:12–13, p. 36
84:14, p. 175
84:14–15, 16, p. 175
84:18, p. 176
84:19, p. 10
84:21, p. 8
84:23, p. 5
84:23–25, pp. 8, 171
84:24, p. 37
84:25, pp. 17, 30
84:25–27, p. 15
84:26–27, p. 9
84:31, p. 169
84:31–34, p. 169
86:8–10, p. 94

86:8–11, p. 101
86:9, 11, p. 102
87:2, p. 132
88:88–91, p. 164
98:32, p. 176
107:40–42, p. 33
107:42, 50, p. 175
107:53–56, p. 157
110:11, pp. 67, 100, 106
110:14, p. 176
113, p. 176
113:1, p. 91
113:1–6, p. 91
113:2, 3, p. 91
113:4, pp. 91, 92, 93, 94
113:5, p. 91
113:6, pp. 49, 92, 94
113:8, p. 94
115:5–6, p. 49
116:1, p. 176
119:4, p. 169
124:38, p. 5
124:39, p. 169
132:1, 34, p. 176
132:38–39, p. 27
132:39, 65, p. 176
133:20–21, p. 156
133:25–27, p. 49
133:25–35, pp. 57, 59
133:26, p. 69
133:26–32, p. 52
133:27, p. 69
133:30, p. 100
133:33–35, p. 60
133:37, p. 102
133:48, 50–51, p. 128
138:39, p. 175

PEARL OF GREAT PRICE

Moses

1:1, p. 176
1:6, p. 33
1:23, p. 32
1:32–33, p. 33
1:34, p. 175
1:41, p. 34

4:1–4, p. 33
5:5–8, p. 33
5:7, p. 21
5:9–12, p. 33
5:18, 20, p. 175
6:2, 25, p. 175
6:64–66, pp. 9, 33
7, p. 5
7:10–11, p. 33
8:12, p. 175
8:23–24, p. 33
8:27, p. 175

Abraham

1:2, p. 175
1:2–3, p. 33
2:6, p. 41
2:9–11, p. 97
2:10, p. 54
3:22–28, p. 33

Joseph Smith–Matthew

1:21–55, p. 132
1:23, pp. 132, 133
1:26, p. 156
1:28, p. 133
1:28–29, p. 132
1:30, p. 137
1:31, p. 101
1:33, p. 164

Joseph Smith–History

1:33–35, p. 161
1:36, pp. 166, 170
1:36–39, p. 165
1:36–41, p. 162
1:38–39, p. 172
1:40, p. 94
1:41, pp. 162, 176
1:69, p. 169
1:71, p. 174

Articles of Faith

4, p. 81
8, p. 32
10, pp. 63, 110, 119

INDEX

Aaronic Priesthood: as the Levitical priesthood, 15, 16; as an inheritance-based priesthood, 15–16; three offices of, in ancient Israel, 16; in today's Church, 16; role of prophets in ancient Israel's, 18

Adam-ondi-Ahman: location identified by Joseph Smith, 156; Joseph Smith on the significance of Adam in God's plan, 156–57; first meeting convened by Adam at, 157; Daniel's vision of Adam's return to, 158–59; events to occur at, 158–59; Joseph Smith on Daniel's vision of Adam's return to, 158–59; Bruce R. McConkie on those who will attend the meeting at, 159; Joseph Smith on the return of the keys of presidency, 159; appearance of Jesus Christ at, 159–60; timing of meeting at, 159–60

Albright, W. F., 76

Alexander the Great, empire of, 151–52

Apocalyptic vision: definition and examples of, 121; dualism in, 122; fulfillment of, 122; types in, 122,

123; vs. metaphor, 122–23; Joseph Smith on understanding, 123

Apostasy. See Israel, Apostasy of

Armageddon: scriptural use of term, 125–26; warfare at Megiddo and, 126–27; natural calamities of, 127; as God's war against the wicked world, 127–28; use of term in conjunction with apocalyptic Old Testament prophecies, 128–29; See also Gog and Magog; Second Coming

Atonement: knowledge of, as a prerequisite for understanding the law of Moses, 14; as the undergirding theme for the sacrificial ordinances of the Mosaic law, 21; necessity of, 23; justice and mercy as basic principles of, 24; as the payment of a penalty, 24; as a reconciliation, 24; satisfying the demands of justice through mercy, 26

Baptism: compared to ritual washing or mikveh, 9; loss of, in Old Testament times, 9–10

Benson, Ezra Taft, on Jesus Christ's

appearance to the Nephites as a
type for his second coming, 130
Bronze, kingdom of. *See*
Nebuchadnezzar's dream
Burnt offerings, 21–22

Christians, ancient Israelites as: in the
Americas, 36; in Palestine, 37–39
Church of Jesus Christ of Latter-day
Saints, The, as the stone cut out of
the mountain without hands,
153–55
Clay, kingdom of. *See*
Nebuchadnezzar's dream
Cowdery, Oliver, 169

David: Jesus Christ as the millennial
King David, 108–11, 118–19;
confusion over identity of
millennial King David, 109; Joseph
Smith on the throne and kingdom
of David, 109; King David as a
model of kingship, 109; as a
metaphor for ideal kingship,
109–10
Dispensation of the fulness of times,
Joseph Smith on, 175
Dualism, 122

Elijah, coming of: fulfillment of
Malachi's prophecy on, 172;
Joseph Smith on, 172, 173
Ephraim, gathering of. *See* Gathering
of Joseph
Esaias, 36
Ezias, 35–36

Gathering of Israel: metaphors used to
describe, 44; repentance and
conversion as prerequisites for, 44;
purposes of, 44–45; Joseph Smith
on the purpose of, 45; Spencer W.
Kimball on, 45; in the latter days,
45–46; Old Testament prophecies
on the latter-day gathering, 46–48;
gathering to covenants as the

essence of, 101. *See also* Scattering
of Israel
Gathering of Joseph: calling of the
tribe of Ephraim to leadership, 50;
impossibility of tracing history of
northern tribes, 50–51; emergence
of descendants of Ephraim, 51–52;
role of Joseph Smith in gathering
descendants of Ephraim and
Manasseh, 51–53; promises made
to descendants of Ephraim and
Manasseh, 60
Gathering of lost ten tribes. *See* Lost
ten tribes
Gathering of the Gentiles: definition of
Gentile, 53–54; adoption of
Gentiles into family of Abraham,
54; John A. Widtsoe on the
adoption of Gentiles into the family
of Abraham, 54; future conversion
of Gentiles and requirements for
membership in the house of Israel,
54–56; James E. Talmage on the
rejection of Israel, 55; blessings
promised to converted Gentiles,
55–56, 60
Gathering of the Jews: Bruce R.
McConkie on the return of the
Jews to Palestine, 56; ancient
promises to Jews, 56–57; sequence
of events for, 57; dedication of
Palestine by Orson Hyde, 57–58;
dedication of western Missouri by
Sidney Rigdon, 58; parallel
circumstances at New Jerusalem
and Old Jerusalem, 58–60;
promises made to the Jews, 60
Gentiles, gathering of the. *See*
Gathering of the Gentiles
Gog and Magog: Ezekiel's vision of,
135–36; fulfillment of prophecies
concerning, 136–37; Nephi's
parallel prophecy of, 137–38;
principal themes of Ezekiel's
prophecy of, 138; post-millennial,
138–39; Joseph Smith on, 139. *See
also* Armageddon; Second Coming

Gold, kingdom of. *See*
Nebuchadnezzar's dream
Good shepherd, Jesus Christ as the,
107–8, 118–19

High priest, as an Aaronic Priesthood
office, 16
Hinckley, Gordon B., on the message
of Old Testament prophets, 12
Hyde, Orson, 57–58

Iron, kingdom of. *See*
Nebuchadnezzar's dream
Isaiah, book of: question of
authorship, 72; typical approach to
dividing, 72; arguments supporting
multiple authorship, 72–73;
prophetic foresight and the
question of authorship, 74;
responses to the question of
authorship, 74–76; as an anthology
of prophetic thought, 76–77; great
value of, 78–79; "likening" the
scriptures, 78–79; historical
background of, 79–80; trusting in
the Lord's saving power as a
principal theme of, 80–81; social
and moral obligations of covenant
people as a principal theme of, 81;
power of God's justice to prevail as
a principal theme of, 81–82;
doctrinal simplicity of, 82; lack of
familiarity with the setting of
Isaiah's day as a challenge to
understanding, 82–84; learning
"the things of the Jews" to
understand, 83–84; understanding
key doctrinal matters as a
prerequisite to comprehending, 84;
lack of understanding of Isaiah's
literary style as a challenge to
comprehending, 84–87;
parallelism in, 85–86; metaphors
in, 86; similes in, 86; mistaking
biblical metaphors for symbolism,
86–87; translation difficulties as a
challenge to understanding, 87–88;
literary style of the Book of
Mormon vs., 88–89; spirit of
prophecy as a prerequisite for
understanding, 89
Isaiah 49:1–6: Joseph Smith as the
servant in, 97–102; servant
prophecies and, 96–97; individual
vs. collective calls to be servants,
97; "called me from the womb,"
98; "in the shadow of his hand
hath he hid me," 98–99; "a
polished shaft . . . in his quiver,"
99; "Thou art my servant,"
99–100; "to bring Jacob again to
him" and "to raise up the tribes of
Jacob, and to restore the preserved
of Israel," 100; "to bring Jacob
again to him, Though Israel be not
gathered," 100–101; "a light to the
Gentiles," 101; Joseph Smith and
co-workers as the fulfillment of the
words of Isaiah, 101–2
Isaiah 49:14–23: as a prophecy about
Zion, 103–4; Gentiles as nursing
fathers and mothers to the house
of Israel, 104–6; gospel to be
carried to the house of Israel by
Gentile missionaries, 105–6; house
of Israel to be restored to promised
lands, 105–6
Israel, apostasy of: beginnings of, 4;
Joseph Smith on the preaching of
the gospel to ancient Israel, 4;
pervasive, continuous nature of, 4;
Joseph Smith on the establishment
of the Church of Jesus Christ in
ancient Israel, 4–5; Joseph Smith
on the law of Moses being added to
the gospel, 5; withdrawal of
Melchizedek Priesthood and its
blessings, 5, 8; difficulty of
determining the exact chronology
of, 5–6; loss of gospel fulness
during Moses' day, 5–6; possible
parallels with apostasy of early
Christian church, 6; condemnation

of Israelites by prophets, 6–7; before and after Moses, 7; effect of withdrawal of priesthood blessings, 8; John Taylor on the withdrawal of priesthood blessings, 8; baptism in Old Testament times, 9–10; loss of gospel light and knowledge, 10–11; Joseph Smith on the loss of gospel knowledge, 11; effect of the loss of gospel light and knowledge on the writings of Old Testament prophets, 11–12; as the consistent message of Old Testament prophets, 12; Gordon B. Hinckley on the message of Old Testament prophets, 12; effect on the Old Testament as a testament of Jesus Christ, 30

Jesse: Jesus Christ as the stem of, 91, 92; latter-day revelation and interpretation of the stem, rod, and root of, 91–92; Hebrew origins of stem, rod, and root, 92; Joseph Smith as the rod and root of, 92–94; ultimate fulfillment of Isaiah's prophecy, 94–95

Jesus Christ: visit to his "other sheep" after being with the children of Lehi, 65–66; records of visits to his "other sheep," 66–67; as the stem of Jesse, 91, 92; as the good shepherd, 107–8, 118–19; as the millennial King David, 108–11, 118–19; Ezra Taft Benson on Christ's appearance to the Nephites as a type for his second coming, 130; appearance at Adam-ondi-Ahman, 159–60

Jesus Christ, Old Testament as a testament of: vs. the Book of Mormon as a testament of Christ, 29; effect of Israel's apostasy on, 30; Joseph Smith on the gospel of Jesus Christ as the only means of salvation, 30; and the intent of the

Old Testament, 30–31; absence of a written record of Christians in ancient Israel and Judah, 31; and the removal of plain and precious things from the Bible, 31–34; Joseph Smith on the veracity of the Bible, 32; modern scriptural evidences of prophetic teachings not included in the Bible, 32–33; role of Joseph Smith in restoring lost truths, 33–34; lack of evidence of Christianity in Mosaic dispensation, 34; Book of Mormon allusions to prophets' teachings absent from the Bible, 34–36

Jews, gathering of. See Gathering of the Jews

Joel, prophecies of: apparent reference to latter days, 161; removal from the context of time and place in which they were revealed, 161; quoted by Moroni to Joseph Smith, 161–62, 163; fulfillment of, in the latter days, 162–63, 164

Joseph, gathering of. See Gathering of Joseph

Joseph, stick of. See Sticks of Joseph and Judah, uniting of

Judah, stick of. See Sticks of Joseph and Judah, uniting of

Justice: as a basic principle of the Atonement, 24; in the law of Moses, 25

Kimball, Spencer W.: on the gathering of Israel, 45; on The Church of Jesus Christ of Latter-day Saints as the stone cut out of the mountain without hands, 153

Last days, sources of erroneous beliefs about, 2

Law of Moses: knowledge of the Atonement as a prerequisite for understanding, 14; power of the Book of Mormon in teaching, 14;

role of, 14–15, 26; as an "attendant" or "custodian," 15; Ten Commandments, 19; civil and religious laws, 19–20; sacrificial ordinances, 20–22; fulfillment of, in Christ, 24–25; justice and mercy in, 25–26; as a prophecy of Christ's mission, 25; obscuring of the law, 37–38; message of Christ in, 38–39; as a preparation for greater revelations to come, 39

Levi, sons of. *See* Sons of Levi

Levitical priesthood: as a lineage-based priesthood, 15; duties of, 16

Lost ten tribes: as a doctrinal question, 62; meaning of "lost," 62; destruction and deportation of northern ten tribes, 62–63; Old Testament prophecies regarding scattering of lost tribes, 63–64; Book of Mormon prophecies regarding scattering and gathering of lost tribes, 64; Christ's visit to his "other sheep" after being with the children of Lehi, 65–66; records of Christ's visit to his "other sheep," 66–67; Joseph Smith on John the Revelator's ministry to, 67–68; history of Lehi's family as a type, 68; restoration of keys of gathering, 69; gathering of, 69–70

Magog. *See* Gog and Magog

Malachi, as a probable pen name, 165–66

Malachi, prophecies of: latter-day focus of, 165; significance of, 165; Moroni quotes part of third chapter to Joseph Smith, 166; messengers in, 166–67; Joseph Smith as one of the messengers in, 167; on the restoration of the sons of Levi to priesthood authority, 167; Joseph Smith on the sons of Levi offering an acceptable sacrifice in the Millennium, 167–69; Joseph Smith on the purification of the sons of Levi, 169; on tithing, 169–70; Moroni quotes chapter four to Joseph Smith, 170; on the cleansing that will accompany the Second Coming, 170–71; Joseph Smith on living the higher law, 171; Joseph Smith on the coming of Elijah, 172, 173; on the coming of Elijah, 172–73

Manasseh, gathering of. *See* Gathering of Joseph

McConkie, Bruce R.: on the return of the Jews to Palestine, 56; on those who will attend the meeting at Adam-ondi-Ahman, 159

Megiddo, 126–27

Melchizedek Priesthood: withdrawal of, in ancient Israel, 5, 8, 15; John Taylor on the withdrawal of, 8; effect of withdrawal of, 8–9; Joseph Smith on prophets and, 10, 17; as the presiding authority in today's Church, 16–17; John Taylor on prophets and, 17; in ancient Israel, 17–18; Joseph Fielding Smith on prophets and, 17–18

Mercy: as a basic principle of the Atonement, 24; in the law of Moses, 25

Metaphors, 86, 122–23

Mosaic law. *See* Law of Moses

Nebuchadnezzar's dream: importance of, to Latter-day Saints, 149; summary of, 149–50; Daniel's interpretation of, 150; as a historical time line, 150–51; Neo-Babylonian empire as the golden head, 151; Persian empire as the silver breast and arms, 151; empire of Alexander the Great and his successors as the belly and thighs of bronze, 151–52; Roman empire as the legs of iron, 152; central message of, 152–53; kingdom of God on earth as the stone cut out of the mountain without hands, 153; Spencer W. Kimball on The Church of Jesus Christ of Latter-day Saints as the stone cut out of the mountain without hands, 153; Brigham Young on The Church of Jesus Christ of Latter-day Saints as the stone cut out of the mountain without hands, 154–55

Neo-Babylonian empire, 151

Neum, 35

Nursing fathers and mothers, 104–6

Packer, Boyd K., on the publication of the Latter-day Saint editions of the scriptures as the uniting of the sticks of Joseph and Judah, 117

Parallelism, 85–86

Persian empire, 151

Pratt, Orson, 36

Priests, in Israel's Aaronic Priesthood, 16

Prophets: John Taylor on the Melchizedek Priesthood and, 17; Joseph Smith on the Melchizedek Priesthood and, 17; Joseph Fielding Smith on the Melchizedek Priesthood and, 17–18; in the hierarchy of the ancient Aaronic system, 18

Restoration: as an explosion of light about the scriptural past, 175; Joseph Smith on, 176

Rigdon, Sidney, 58

Rod of Jesse. See Jesse

Roman empire, 152

Root of Jesse. See Jesse

Sacrificial ordinances: as ancient Israel's principal temple ordinances, 20–21; focus of, 21; loss of true meaning of, after Moses' time, 21; as symbolic of the

Atonement, 21; burnt offerings, 21–22; sin and trespass offerings, 22; as a type, 22; well-being offerings, 22

Scattering of Israel: expulsion from a choice land as a sign of God's displeasure, 41–42; northern ten tribes, 42–43; descendants of Lehi, 43; Jews, 43–44. See also Gathering of Israel

Scattering of lost ten tribes. See Lost ten tribes

Sealing power, restoration of, 172–73

Second Coming: Ezra Taft Benson on Christ's appearance to the Nephites as a type for, 130; parallel events with those preceding Christ's appearance to the Nephites, 130–32; wars preceding, 132–33; absence of scriptural evidence for battle at time of, 133; Joseph Smith on, 156; public nature of, 156; cleansing to occur at time of, 170–71. See also Adam-ondi-Ahman; Armageddon; Gog and Magog

Shepherds, 107–8

Silver, kingdom of. See Nebuchadnezzar's dream

Similes, 86

Sin offerings, 22

Smith, Joseph: on the preaching of the gospel to ancient Israel, 4; on the establishment of the Church of Jesus Christ in ancient Israel, 4–5; on the building up of Zion in all ages, 5; on the law of Moses being added to the gospel, 5; on prophets and the Melchizedek Priesthood, 10, 17; on the loss of gospel knowledge, 11; on making one's calling and election sure, 12; on the gospel of Jesus Christ as the only means of salvation, 30; on the veracity of the Bible, 32; role in restoring lost truths, 33–34; on the purpose of gathering Israel, 45;

role in gathering descendants of Ephraim and Manasseh, 51–53; on John the Revelator's ministry to the lost ten tribes, 67–68; as the rod and root of Jesse, 92–94; on the throne and kingdom of David, 109; on understanding apocalyptic vision, 123; on post-millennial Gog and Magog, 139; identifies location of Adam-ondi-Ahman, 156; on the public nature of the Second Coming, 156; on the significance of Adam in God's plan, 156–57; on Daniel's vision of Adam's return to Adam-ondi-Ahman, 158–59; on the return of the keys of presidency at Adam-ondi-Ahman, 159; as one of the messengers referred to by Malachi, 167; on the sons of Levi offering an acceptable sacrifice during the Millennium, 167–69; on the purification of the sons of Levi, 169; on living the higher law, 171; on the coming of Elijah, 172, 173; on the dispensation of the fulness of times, 175; Old Testament people illuminated by the teachings of, 175–76; on the Restoration, 176; significance of the ministry of, 176–77. *See also* Isaiah 49:1–6

Smith, Joseph Fielding, on prophets and the Melchizedek Priesthood, 17–18

Sons of Levi: acceptable sacrifice to be offered by, 167–69; Joseph Smith on the purification of, 169

Stem of Jesse. *See* Jesse

Sticks of Joseph and Judah, uniting of: dual meaning of, 112–13; meanings of Hebrew word for stick, 113; restoration of the house of Israel as the central message of Ezekiel's prophecy of, 113–14; as a prophecy of the coming together of two sacred records, 114–16; coming together of two sacred records as a central event in the restoration of the house of Israel, 115–17; Boyd K. Packer on the publication of the Latter-day Saint editions of the scriptures as, 117; reunification of the nations of Israel and Judah, 117–18

Stone cut out of the mountain without hands. *See* Nebuchadnezzar's dream

Sun/Son of righteousness, 170–71

Talmage, James E., on Israel's rejection of the invitation to the feast, 55

Taylor, John, on prophets and the Melchizedek Priesthood, 17

Temple in Jerusalem, Ezekiel's vision of: apocalyptic nature of, 141–42; re-entry of the glory of the Lord, 142, 146; vs. his earlier vision, 142–43; altar scene, 143; temple entrance scene, 143; division of land among the tribes, 143–44; as a representation of the millennial condition of the house of Israel, 144; limitations imposed by the doctrinal understanding of those who would read it, 144–45; millennial construction and use of the temple by Latter-day Saints, 145–47

Ten Commandments, as the fundamental rule for any community, 19

Tithing, 169

Trespass offerings, 22

Types, 122, 123

Wars. *See* Armageddon; Gog and Magog; Second Coming

Well-being offerings, 22

Whitmer, John, 67

Widtsoe, John A., on the adoption of Gentiles into the family of Abraham, 54

Young, Brigham, on The Church of
    Jesus Christ of Latter-day Saints as
    the stone cut out of the mountain
    without hands, 154–55

Zenock, 35–36
Zenos, 35–36
Zion: Joseph Smith on the building up
    of Zion in all ages, 5; multiple
    meanings of, 103; millennial, 119